AF442731

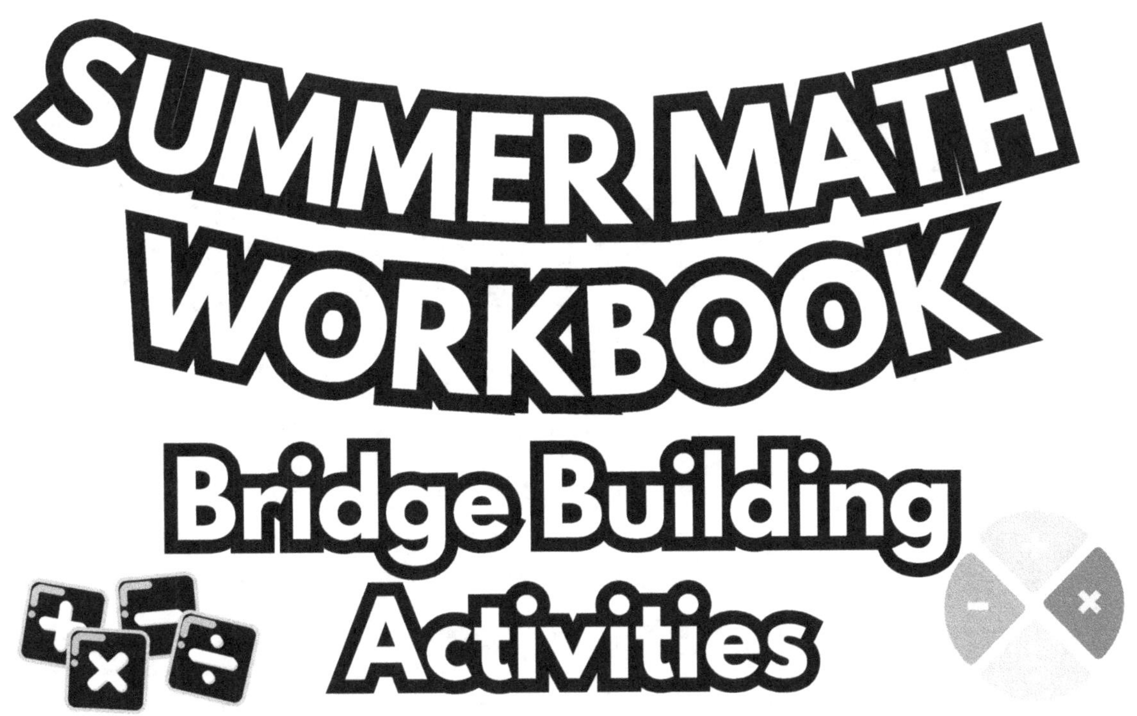

SUMMER MATH
WORKBOOK
Bridge Building
Activities

Bridge
Name

Grade
1 → 2
SUMMER MATH WORKBOOK
Bridge Building Activities
Number Sense
Addition and Subtraction
Place Value

Grade
2 → 3
SUMMER MATH WORKBOOK
Bridge Building Activities
Number Sense
Addition and Subtraction
Place Value

Grade
3 → 4
SUMMER MATH WORKBOOK
Bridge Building Activities
Number Sense
Addition and Subtraction
Place Value

Grade
4 → 5
SUMMER MATH WORKBOOK
Bridge Building Activities
Multiplication and Division
Place Value and Units
Fractions and Geometry

Grade
5 → 6
SUMMER MATH WORKBOOK
Bridge Building Activities
Multiplication and Division
Factors and Multiples
Fractions and Geometry

Grade
6 → 7
SUMMER MATH WORKBOOK
Bridge Building Activities
Arithmetic
Algebra
Geometry and Statistics

Grade
7 → 8
SUMMER MATH WORKBOOK
Bridge Building Activities
Ratio and Percentage
Algebra and Cartesian Plane
Geometry and Statistics

Grade
8 → 9
SUMMER MATH WORKBOOK
Bridge Building Activities
Ratio and Percentage
Algebra
Geometry and Graphing

Grade
9 → 10
SUMMER MATH WORKBOOK
Bridge Building Activities
Factoring and Distributing
Algebra
Geometry and Graphing

<u>Introduction</u>

As parents and educators, we understand the pivotal role that mathematics plays in shaping a child's academic journey and future success. Yet, the path to mathematical proficiency can often seem daunting, filled with challenges and complexities. That's where the transformative power of Summer Bridge Building Activities books comes into play, illuminating the way forward with clarity, precision, and purpose.

Summer vacation is a time for rest and relaxation, but it also presents the risk of the "summer slide," where students lose some of the academic gains they made during the school year. Summer Bridge Building Activities books are specifically designed to tackle this challenge, ensuring that your child stays academically engaged and prepared for the upcoming school year. These books provide a seamless bridge from one grade to the next, reinforcing essential skills and introducing new concepts that will give your child a head start.

Imagine your child eagerly diving into the pages of a Summer Bridge Building Activities book, greeted by clear, engaging content that demystifies complex mathematical concepts. With each turn of the pages, they embark on a journey of discovery, encountering thoughtfully curated practice questions that reinforce learning and sharpen problem-solving skills. As they unveil the answers to those questions, a sense of accomplishment blossoms within them — a tangible reward for their hard work and dedication.

Summer Bridge Building Activities books transcend traditional educational tools; they are meticulously crafted to build a deep and enduring understanding of mathematics. These books follow a sequential and logical progression, starting from fundamental principles and advancing to sophisticated problem-solving strategies. Each chapter is designed to build on the previous one, ensuring a solid and comprehensive foundation for future learning.

Parents, we yearn for nothing more than to see our children thrive academically and personally. We want to witness the spark of inspiration ignited within them as they overcome academic challenges with confidence and poise. Summer Bridge Building Activities books serve as indispensable partners in this noble endeavor, offering not just practice questions but the keys to unlocking a world of academic and personal opportunities.

Visualize the pride on your child's face as they master a challenging math concept, the joy they experience when their efforts yield results, and the confidence they gain with each success. These pages are designed to make learning math a positive, enriching, and deeply rewarding experience that will benefit them throughout their academic journey and beyond.

For educators, Summer Bridge Building Activities books are invaluable allies in the quest to cultivate mathematical proficiency in the classroom. Accompanied by comprehensive guides and readily available answers, instructors can focus on mentoring and nurturing their students, secure in the knowledge that these books provide a robust framework for effective learning.

Within the pages of Summer Bridge Building Activities books lies not just the promise of academic excellence, but the seeds of a brighter future. By integrating these resources into your child's summer routine, you are bestowing upon them the gifts of confidence, curiosity, and a lifelong love of learning.

Invest in your child's future today with Summer Bridge Building Activities books — because every great journey begins with a single step, and this step can change everything. Keep the momentum of learning alive over the summer, and watch your child soar to new academic heights.

Contents

Grade
7 - 9
PRE ALGEBRA
WORKBOOK
BRIDGE BUILDING
ACTIVITIES
Equations, Inequalities
and Expressions
Linear Equations
Graphing and Slope
System of Equations
Quadratic Equations

Grade
6 - 8
PRE ALGEBRA
WORKBOOK
BRIDGE BUILDING
ACTIVITIES
Equations
One Side and Two Sides
Verbal Algebra
Expressions
Linear Equations and Slope
Order of Operations

Grade
5 - 6
PRE ALGEBRA
WORKBOOK
BRIDGE BUILDING
ACTIVITIES
Integers, Mixed Numbers
Decimals and Fractions
Place Value
Exponents and Roots
Percentage and Ratio
Word Problems

PRE ALGEBRA
WORKBOOK
for
Beginners
Integers
Fractions, Mixed Numbers
Place Value
Exponents and Roots
Percentage
Ratio Conversion

PRE ALGEBRA
WORKBOOK
for
Adults
Integers
Percent and Ratio
Equations, Inequalities
Expressions
Order of Operations

Grade
7 - 8
PRE ALGEBRA
WORKBOOK
BRIDGE BUILDING
ACTIVITIES
Equations, Inequalities
and Expressions
Verbal Algebra
Expressions
Percent and Ratio
Word Problems

Grade
9 - 10
PRE ALGEBRA
WORKBOOK
BRIDGE BUILDING
ACTIVITIES
Equations and Inequalities
Verbal Algebra
Linear and Quadratic
Equations
System of Equations
Polynomials

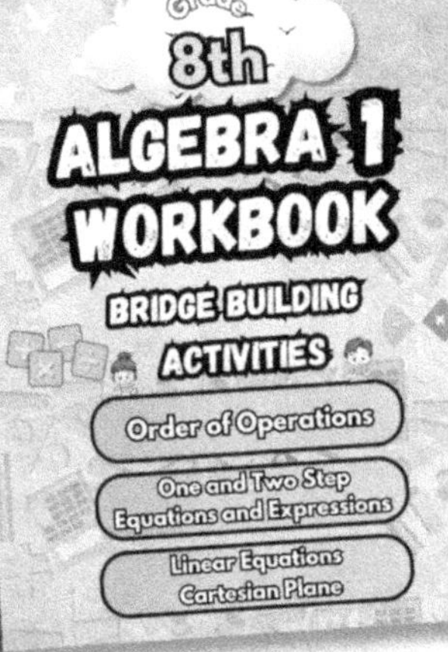
Grade
8th
ALGEBRA 1
WORKBOOK
BRIDGE BUILDING
ACTIVITIES
Order of Operations
One and Two Step
Equations and Expressions
Linear Equations
Cartesian Plane

Grade
7 - 9
ALGEBRA 1
WORKBOOK
BRIDGE BUILDING
ACTIVITIES
Integers
Order of Operations
One and Multi Step
Equations and Expressions
Linear, Quadratic Equations
Equations One Side, Two Sides

<u>**Exponents**</u>

An exponent tells us how many times a number (called the base) is multiplied by itself. It is written as a superscript to the right of the base number. For example, in 2^3, 2 is the base and 3 is the exponent.

Rules:

1. **Product Rule**: When multiplying powers with the same base, add the exponents.

$$a^m \times a^n = a^{m+n}$$

For example:

$$2^3 = 2 \times 2 \times 2 = 8$$

$$3^2 \times 3^4 = 3^{2+4} = 3^6 = 3 \times 3 \times 3 \times 3 \times 3 \times 3 = 729$$

2. **Quotient Rule**: When dividing powers with the same base, subtract the exponents.

$$a^m \div a^n = a^{m-n}$$

For example:

$$5^3 \div 5^2 = 5^{3-2} = 5^1 = 5$$

3. **Power of a Power Rule**: When raising a power to another power, multiply the exponents.

$$(a^m)^n = a^{mn}$$

For example:

$$(2^2)^3 = 2^{2\times3} = 2^6 = 64$$

4. **Power of a Product Rule**: When raising a product to a power, distribute the power to each factor.

$$(ab)^n = a^n \times b^n$$

For example:

$$(2 \times 3)^2 = 2^2 \times 3^2 = 4 \times 9 = 36$$

5. **Power of a Quotient Rule**: When raising a quotient to a power, distribute the power to the numerator and denominator separately.

$$\left(\frac{a}{b}\right)^n = \frac{a^n}{b^n}$$

For example:

$$\left(\frac{4}{2}\right)^3 = \frac{4^3}{2^3} = \frac{64}{8} = 8$$

6. **Zero Exponent Rule**: Any nonzero number raised to the power of zero equals 11.

$$a^0 = 1$$

For example:

$$7^0 = 1$$

7. **Negative Exponent Rule**: A negative exponent means the reciprocal of the base raised to the positive exponent.

$$a^{-n} = \frac{1}{a^n}$$

For example:

$$2^{-3} = \frac{1}{2^3} = \frac{1}{8}$$

To evaluate expressions with exponents, we can use:

- **Repeated Multiplication**: Perform the multiplication indicated by the exponent.

- **Using the Rules of Exponents**: Apply the appropriate rule to simplify expressions involving exponents.

Square Roots

The square root of a number is a value that, when multiplied by itself, gives the original number. It's denoted by the symbol $\sqrt{\ }$.

For example, the square root of 9 is 3 because 3 * 3 = 9.

Cube Roots

The cube root of a number is a value that, when multiplied by itself twice, gives the original number. It's denoted by the symbol $\sqrt[3]{\ }$.

For example, the cube root of 8 is 2 because 2 * 2 * 2 = 8.

Exponents

Convert the values.

1. $5^{-3} =$ _______________

2. $14^{-3} =$ _______________

3. $8^{-2} =$ _______________

4. $7^{2} =$ _______________

5. $3^{3} =$ _______________

6. $7^{-2} =$ _______________

7. $13^{4} =$ _______________

8. $12^{3} =$ _______________

9. $19^{3} =$ _______________

10. $9^{3} =$ _______________

11. $10^{-2} =$ _______________

12. $16^{-2} =$ _______________

13. $17^{4} =$ _______________

14. $3^{2} =$ _______________

15. $18^{-2} =$ _______________

16. $10^{-3} =$ _______________

17. $6^{2} =$ _______________

18. $13^{-2} =$ _______________

19. $14^{-2} =$ _______________

20. $19^{2} =$ _______________

21. $9^{-3} =$ _________________

22. $7^{3} =$ _________________

23. $1^{-3} =$ _________________

24. $18^{-3} =$ _________________

25. $10^{4} =$ _________________

26. $18^{3} =$ _________________

27. $11^{4} =$ _________________

28. $20^{4} =$ _________________

29. $17^{3} =$ _________________

30. $13^{-3} =$ _________________

Square and Cube Roots

Calculate the root of each value.

1. $\sqrt[3]{8,000}$ = _____________

2. $\sqrt[3]{1,000}$ = _____________

3. $\sqrt{121}$ = _____________

4. $\sqrt[3]{512}$ = _____________

5. $\sqrt[3]{64}$ = _____________

6. $\sqrt{9}$ = _____________

7. $\sqrt{361}$ = _____________

8. $\sqrt{961}$ = _____________

9. $\sqrt{1}$ = _____________

10. $\sqrt{529}$ = _____________

11. $\sqrt[3]{27}$ = _____________

12. $\sqrt{16}$ = _____________

13. $\sqrt{100}$ = _______________

14. $\sqrt[3]{1,728}$ = _______________

15. $\sqrt[3]{8}$ = _______________

16. $\sqrt{4}$ = _______________

17. $\sqrt{36}$ = _______________

18. $\sqrt[3]{1,331}$ = _______________

19. $\sqrt[3]{5,832}$ = _______________

20. $\sqrt{9,801}$ = _______________

21. $\sqrt[3]{125}$ = _______________

22. $\sqrt[3]{216}$ = _______________

23. $\sqrt{2,209}$ = _______________

24. $\sqrt{576}$ = _______________

25. $\sqrt{8{,}100} =$ _______________

26. $\sqrt[3]{10{,}648} =$ _______________

27. $\sqrt{64} =$ _______________

28. $\sqrt{3{,}136} =$ _______________

29. $\sqrt{169} =$ _______________

30. $\sqrt{5{,}929} =$ _______________

31. $\sqrt[3]{729} =$ _______________

32. $\sqrt[3]{1} =$ _______________

33. $\sqrt{81} =$ _______________

34. $\sqrt{196} =$ _______________

35. $\sqrt[3]{4{,}913} =$ _______________

36. $\sqrt{8{,}649} =$ _______________

Factors

1. 28

2. 8

3. 70

4. 1

5. 3

6. 42

7. 6

8. 75 ____

9. 88 ____

10. 9 ____

11. 94 ____

12. 84 ____

13. 96 ____

14. 66 ____

15. 48 ____

16. 98 ____

17. 7 ____

18. 71 ____

19. 20 ____

20. 55 ____

21. 12 ____

22. 79 ____

23. 14 ____

24. 44 ____

25. 63 ____

26. 65 ____

27. 15 ____

28. 2 ____

Multiples

1. 23 _______________________________

2. 15 _______________________________

3. 22 _______________________________

4. 4 _______________________________

5. 81 _______________________________

6. 95 _______________________________

7. 87 _______________________________

8. 48 ______________________________

9. 38 ______________________________

10. 2 ______________________________

11. 60 ______________________________

12. 3 ______________________________

13. 1 ______________________________

14. 20 ______________________________

15. 7

16. 59

17. 70

18. 9

19. 28

20. 14

21. 18

22. 61 ____

23. 6 ____

24. 10 ____

25. 8 ____

26. 34 ____

27. 30 ____

28. 84 ____

<u>**Greatest Common Factors**</u>

The Greatest Common Factor (GCF), also known as the Greatest Common Divisor (GCD), of two or more numbers is the largest number that divides each of the numbers without leaving a remainder. It is the greatest number that is a common factor of the given numbers.

There are two main methods to find the GCF:

- Prime Factorization,
- Using Factors.

Let's find GCF of 44, and 33 using factors:

- List all the factors of each number:

Factors of 44: 1, 2, 4, 11, 22, 44

Factors of 33: 1, 3, 11, 33

- Identify and chose the common factors:

The common factor between 44 and 33 is 11.

Greatest Common Factor

Find the greatest common factor.

1. 28 ____ ___
    84 ____

2. 24 ____ ___
    27 ____

3. 96 ____ ___
    84 ____

4. 14 ____ ___
    86 ____

5. 77 ____ ___
    44 ____

6. 88
22

7. 50
28

8. 66
88

9. 55
66

10. 11
22

11. 55
77

12. 45 _______________________________ ___

96 _______________________________

13. 36 _______________________________ ___

63 _______________________________

14. 36 _______________________________ ___

75 _______________________________

15. 66 _______________________________ ___

30 _______________________________

16. 50 _______________________________ ___

30 _______________________________

17. 94 _______________________________ ___

84 _______________________________

18.   66
55

19.   85
60

20.   80
95

21.   28
35

22.   100
54

23.   63
21

<u>**Prime Numbers**</u>

A prime number is a natural number greater than 1 that has no positive divisors other than 1 and itself.

Rules for Prime Numbers:

1. Prime numbers are greater than 1.

2. Prime numbers have only two distinct positive divisors: 1 and the number itself.

3. Prime numbers are not divisible by any other number except 1 and themselves.

4. 2 is the only even prime number.

Methods for Identifying Prime Numbers:

1. Trial Division: Check divisibility by all numbers up to the square root of the number.

2. Sieve of Eratosthenes: Generate a list of prime numbers up to a certain limit by eliminating multiples of prime numbers.

3. Using Prime Factorization: Factorize the number into its prime factors.

For Example: Let's analyze a few numbers to determine if they are prime or not:

Number	Is Prime?
7	Yes
8	No (divisible by 2)
19	Yes
65	No (divisible by 5)
221	No (divisible by 13)

Prime Numbers

List the prime factors for each number. Is the number prime?

1. 38 = ______________________

2. 7 = ______________________

3. 49 = ______________________

4. 19 = ______________________

5. 9 = ______________________

6. 4 = ______________________

7. 83 = ______________________

8. 46 = ______________________

9. 89 = ______________________

10. 1 = ______________________

11. 78 = ______________________

12. 43 = ______________________

13. 64 = ______________________

14. 3 = ______________________

15. 58 = _______________

16. 35 = _______________

17. 22 = _______________

18. 88 = _______________

19. 26 = _______________

20. 54 = _______________

21. 79 = _______________

22. 36 = _______________

23. 8 = _______________

24. 48 = _______________

25. 6 = _______________

26. 17 = _______________

27. 63 = _______________

28. 87 = _______________

29. 25 = _______________

30. 96 = _______________

Operations with Integers

Positive and negative integers are whole numbers that can represent quantities greater than zero and less than zero, respectively.

Positive Integers: Positive integers are whole numbers greater than zero. They are denoted by the numbers 1,2,3,4...

Negative Integers: Negative integers are whole numbers less than zero. They are denoted by placing a negative sign ("-") before the numbers, such as $-1,-2,-3,-4,...$

The positive integers are used to represent the number of objects, scores, etc. whereas the negative integers can be used to represent debt, losses, temperatures below freezing points, etc.

Let's solve some problems:

1. 6 – (– 8) – 9

- Start by simplifying within the parentheses:

$$- (-8) \text{ becomes } 8.$$

- Rewrite the expression with the simplified part:

$$6 + 8 - 9.$$

- Now perform addition and subtraction from left to right:

$$6 + 8 = 1\,4, \text{ then } 14 - 9 = 5$$

2. (– 5) – (– 3) + 10

$$(-5) + 3 + 10$$

$$(-5) + 3 = -2, \text{ then } -2 + 10 = 8$$

Positive and Negative Integers

Evaluate.

1. $(-6) - (-5) + 2 =$

2. $(-5) + (-3) =$

3. $(-10) + 5 + (-1) =$

4. $(-7) - 7 + (-4) =$

5. $1 - 8 + 8 =$

6. $(-4) + 1 =$

7. $(-5) - (-5) + 9 =$

8. $2 - 4 + 7 =$

9. $8 + (-3) =$

10. $(-9) + 5 + (-9) =$

11. $(-7) + (-8) - 9 =$

12. $(-8) - (-8) - (-3) =$

13. $2 + 9 - 8 =$

14. $(-3) - 5 =$

15. $(-4) - 1 + (-3) =$

16. $8 + 5 - 3 =$

17. $1 - 8 + 3 =$

18. $10 - 6 + (-4) =$

19. $(-1) + (-6) - 10 =$

20. $9 - 5 + 10 =$

21. $(-8) - 10 + (-7) =$

22. $8 + (-2) - 9 =$

23. $(-4) + 8 + (-9) =$

24. $(-7) - (-9) =$

25. $7 + (-9) - 7 =$

26. $(-9) - 1 + (-2) =$

27. $9 - 10 + 7 =$

28. $2 + 5 - 2 =$

Order of Operations (PEMDAS)

The order of operations, often remembered by the acronym PEMDAS, stands for:

- **Parentheses**: Perform operations inside parentheses first.
- **Exponents**: Evaluate exponents (powers and roots) next.
- **Multiplication and Division**: Perform multiplication and division from left to right.
- **Addition and Subtraction:** Perform addition and subtraction from left to right.

The order of operations helps to clarify which operations should be performed first in a mathematical expression to ensure consistent and accurate results.

- **Parentheses**: Evaluate expressions within parentheses first. If there are nested parentheses, start with the innermost ones and work your way out.

    1. Example: $2 \times (3 + 4) = 2 \times 7 = 14$

- **Exponents**: Evaluate expressions with exponents (powers and roots) next.

    1. Example: $2^3 + 4 = 8 + 4 = 12$

- **Multiplication and Division**: Perform multiplication and division from left to right.

    1. Example: $2 \times 3 + 4 = 6 + 4 = 10$

    2. Example: $6 \div 2 \times 3 = 3 \times 3 = 9$

- **Addition and Subtraction**: Perform addition and subtraction from left to right.

    1. Example: $2 + 3 \times 4 = 2 + 12 = 14$

    2. Example: $10 - 4 \div 2 = 10 - 2 = 8$

Order of Operations (PEMDAS)

Evaluate Expressions.

1. 5 + 1 + 3 =

2. 5 + 3 + 10 =

3. 6 + 2 + 6 + 9 =

4. 10 + 1 + 3 + 9 =

5. 10 + 2 + 4 + 10 =

6. 9 + 10 + 6 + 9 =

7. 9 + 2 + 3 =

8. 2 + 5 + 5 =

9. $5 + 5 + 5 + 6 =$

10. $1 + 9 + 7 + 7 =$

11. $4 + 4 + 9 + 2 =$

12. $1 + 4 + 3 =$

13. $7 + 3 + 6 =$

14. $9 + 8 + 8 + 7 =$

15. $1 + 4 + 5 =$

16. $7 + 7 + 6 + 2 =$

17. $2 + 3 + 1 + 6 =$

18. $1 + 7 + 1 =$

19. $5 + 4 + 10 + 4 =$

20. $2 + 4 + 9 =$

21. $1 + 1 + 7 + 10 =$

22. $2 + 6 + 2 + 10 =$

23. $7 + 4 + 7 + 8 =$

24. $9 + 5 + 1 =$

25. $2 + 4 + 3 =$

26. $1 + 5 + 2 =$

27. $2 + 8 + 6 + 10 =$

28. $8 + 2 + 3 =$

<u>Solving Equations (One Side)</u>

Solving one-step equations involves performing a single operation to isolate the variable and find its value.

Let's solve an equation step by step: $16 + x = 31$

1. Identify the Goal:

     The goal is to isolate the variable x on one side of the equation.

2. Simplify the Equation: Combine like terms on both sides of the equation, if necessary.

     The equation is already simplified.

3. Undo Addition or Subtraction: If there's addition or subtraction involving the variable, undo it by performing the opposite operation on both sides of the equation.

     Since x is being added to 16, we'll undo this operation by subtracting 16 from both sides of the equation:
     $$16 + x - 16 = 31 - 16$$

4. Isolate the Variable: Ensure that the variable is alone on one side of the equation.

     $$x = 15$$

5. Check Your Solution: Substitute the value of x back into the original equation to verify that it satisfies the equation.

     $$16 + 15 = 31$$

     $$31 = 31$$

The equation is balanced.

Solving Equations: (One Side)

Solve the equations for the variable.

1. $40 = x \times 10$

2. $56 = 14 \times x$

3. $1 = x - 18$

4. $24 = x + 15$

5. $26 = x + 8$

6. $17 - x = 8$

7. $18 \times x = 144$

8. $88 = x \times 11$

9. $16 - x = 3$

10. $2 - x = 0$

11. $2 = 20 \div x$

12. $1 = x \div 12$

13. $18 + x = 20$

14. $11 + x = 18$

15. $96 = x \times 8$

16. $13 = 182 \div x$

17. $7 = x - 8$

18. $x \times 9 = 144$

19. $1 = x - 9$

20. $x + 11 = 26$

21. $105 \div x = 15$

22. $11 = x - 7$

23. $4 \times x = 8$

24. $16 \times x = 224$

25. $29 = x + 19$

26. $18 - x = 6$

27. $15 = 1 + x$

28. $x + 2 = 5$

Solving One-Step Equations

Solving one-step equations involves finding the value of the variable that makes the equation true. In a one-step equation, there is only one operation (addition, subtraction, multiplication, or division) performed on the variable.

The goal is to isolate the variable on one side of the equation by performing inverse operations.

For example:

Given the equation $6 = -3z$, where we want to solve for z.

The given equation is already in the form of a one-step equation, with z being multiplied by -3.

To isolate z, we need to perform the inverse operation of multiplication, which is division.

Divide both sides by -3:

$$\frac{6}{-3} = \frac{-3z}{-3}$$

Simplify:

$$-2 = z$$

So, the solution to the equation is $z = -2$.

When we substitute the value of $z = -2$ back into the original equation, $6 = -3(-2)$, it simplifies to $6 = 6$. This confirms that our solution is correct because it satisfies the original equation.

One-Step Equations

Solve for the variable.

1. $4(1 + k) = 24$

2. $1.5 = 9 \div m$

3. $10.9 = b + (9 \div b)$

4. $2 \times (k - 1) = 12$

5. $29 = a \times 5 - 6$

6. $1 \div m = 0.3$

7. $24 = x \times 2 + 6$

8. $5 = k + 3$

9. $30 = (3 \times b) + 9$

10. $18 = 3m - m$

11. $12 = 6 \times (a - 5)$

12. $k + 5 = 12$

13. $37 = a \times 5 - 3$

14. $45 = 10a - a$

15. $10.1 = 10 + (a \div 8)$

16. $8 + (s \div 4) = 10$

17. $6 + (2 \times b) = 24$

18. $63 = 9z + 9$

19. $9 = s \div 1$

20. $7 + (y - 6) = 10$

21. $2 = s \div 4$

22. $9 \times (k - 7) = -45$

23. $-4 = k - 10$

24. $10 \div y = 2.5$

25. $y \times 1 + 6 = 15$

26. $30 = b \times 2 + b$

27. $z \times 3 - 4 = 26$

28. $72 = s \times 7 + s$

29. $y - 9 = -3$

30. $3(2 - x) = -6$

31. $6.7 = x + (4 \div x)$

32. $10b - b = 63$

Solving Two-Step Equations

Solving two-step equations involves finding the value of the variable that makes the equation true. In a two-step equation, two operations (addition, subtraction, multiplication, or division) are performed on the variable.

The goal is to isolate the variable on one side of the equation by performing inverse operations in the reverse order of operations.

For example:

Given the equation $18 = (10 + b) - 2$, where we want to solve for b.

To solve for b, we need to undo the operations that have been performed on b.

1. Undo the subtraction by adding 2 to both sides:

$$18 + 2 = (10 + b) - 2 + 2$$
$$20 = 10 + b$$

2. Undo the addition by subtracting 10 from both sides:

$$20 - 10 = 10 + b - 10$$
$$10 = b$$

So, the solution to the equation is $b = 10$

Let's substitute $b = 10$ back into the original equation to verify if it satisfies the equation:

Original equation:

$$18 = (10 + b) - 2:$$

Substitute $b = 10$:

$$18 = (10 + 10) - 2$$

simplify:

$$18 = 20 - 2$$
$$18 = 18$$

Since the equation simplifies to 18 =1 8, it confirms that our solution $b = 10$ is correct.

Two-Step Equations

Solve for the variable.

1. $10 = 8y + 2$

2. $10b + 6 + (9b - 3) = 60$

3. $8 + (9b + 9) = 71$

4. $9 + (5x + 8) = 52$

5. $7x + x = 24$

6. $5 = 1 \times k - 3$

7. $144 = (6y)^2$

8. $3 + (2x + 4) = 15$

9. $19 = s + 3 + s$

10. $28 = 5k + 3$

11. $16 = 4y - 10 + 9y$

12. $z + 6 + 10z = 28$

13. $38 = 7x + 8x + 4x$

14. $15 = m + 3 + 5m$

15. $5 - (1 \times s) = -1$

16. $b^2 + b - 7 = 103$

17. $6z + 6z - 5 = 31$

18. $(10 \times y) - 1 = 69$

19. $(3 - s) \times 6 = -12$

20. $6 \times (8 + y) = 60$

21. $29 = 5 \times z - 1$

22. $102 = 6 \times (9 + s)$

23. $7 = z + 2$

24. $12 = b + 2 + 9b$

25. $88 = 8 \times (1 + k)$

26. $9k + 7k - 7 = 153$

27. $-70 = (1 - b) \times 10$

28. $10s + 7s + s = 162$

29. $2z + 4z + 5z = 11$

30. $(1 \times y) + 10 = 17$

31. $31 = 3 \times z + 7$

32. $4 \times (10 - x) = 28$

Solving Inequalities

Inequalities are mathematical expressions that compare the relative sizes of two values. They are used to express relationships where one quantity is:

- "<" (less than),
- ">" (greater than),
- "<=" (less than or equal to),
- ">=" (greater than or equal to),
- and "≠" (not equal to) another quantity.

For example:

$$y + -10 \leq -8$$

To isolate y, we need to get rid of the constant term -10. Since -10 is being subtracted from y, we can undo this operation by adding 10 to both sides of the inequality:

$$y - 10 + 10 \leq -8 + 10$$

$$y \leq 2$$

To check the solution:

$$2 - 10 \leq -8$$

$$-8 = -8$$

The inequality is true when $y = 2$

Solving Inequalities

1. $3 < 2 - z$

2. $6 > 7 + x$

3. $-7 \leq -9 + z$

4. $8 \leq 2 - z$

5.

$$z - -9 \leq 7$$

6.

$$x + 2 \leq -2$$

7.

$$-6 - z < 9$$

8.

$$x + 2 > 5$$

9.

$$-5 + k < -10$$

10.

$$7 - x \geq 8$$

11.

$$z + 8 \leq -4$$

12.

$$7 < 2 - x$$

13.

$$x - {-4} \leq 1$$

14.

$$-9 \leq -8 + m$$

15.

$$x + 5 \leq 5$$

16.

$$9 > 8 - k$$

17.

$$z + -2 > -9$$

18.

$$7 \geq k - 6$$

19.

$$-4 > 7 + m$$

20.

$$9 \leq 8 - z$$

Ratio and Proportion

A proportional relationship between two quantities exists when they have a constant ratio or when one is a multiple of the other. In other words, if we increase one quantity, the other quantity will increase or decrease by the same factor. For example, if we double one quantity, the other quantity will also double.

Let's solve a problem:

$$\frac{\square}{9} = \frac{8}{18}$$

Step 1: Cross Multiply: Cross multiply by multiplying the numerator of one fraction by the denominator of the other, and vice versa:

$$x \times 18 = 9 \times 8$$

Step 2: Solve for the Unknown: Perform the multiplication on both sides of the equation:

$$18x = 72$$

Step 3: Divide Both Sides by the Coefficient of the Unknown: To isolate x, divide both sides of the equation by the coefficient of x, which is 18:

$$\frac{18x}{18} = \frac{72}{18}$$

$$x = 4$$

Step 4: Verify Check your solution by substituting $x = 4$ back into the original equation:

$$\frac{4}{9} = \frac{8}{18}$$

Since both sides are equal, the solution $x = 4$ is correct.

Proportional Relationship

Solve each Ratio and Proportion.

1. $\dfrac{4}{5} = \dfrac{}{30}$

2. $\dfrac{}{10} = \dfrac{15}{30}$

3. $\dfrac{}{2} = \dfrac{6}{12}$

4. $\dfrac{7}{8} = \dfrac{}{72}$

5. $\dfrac{2}{} = \dfrac{18}{27}$

6. $\dfrac{2}{6} = \dfrac{}{48}$

7. $\dfrac{6}{} = \dfrac{36}{42}$

8. $\dfrac{5}{} = \dfrac{20}{48}$

9. $\dfrac{2}{} = \dfrac{8}{16}$

10. $\dfrac{2}{9} = \dfrac{18}{}$

11. $\dfrac{}{6} = \dfrac{9}{54}$

12. $\dfrac{1}{5} = \dfrac{9}{}$

13. $\dfrac{1}{} = \dfrac{10}{110}$

14. $\dfrac{6}{9} = \dfrac{}{54}$

15. $\dfrac{4}{7} = \dfrac{}{21}$

16. $\dfrac{1}{3} = \dfrac{2}{}$

17. $\dfrac{}{8} = \dfrac{20}{32}$

18. $\dfrac{1}{} = \dfrac{3}{6}$

19. $\dfrac{8}{} = \dfrac{16}{24}$

20. $\dfrac{2}{} = \dfrac{4}{8}$

21. $\dfrac{3}{7} = \dfrac{21}{}$

22. $\dfrac{2}{11} = \dfrac{18}{}$

23. $\dfrac{}{6} = \dfrac{8}{24}$

24. $\dfrac{3}{9} = \dfrac{27}{}$

25. $\dfrac{2}{} = \dfrac{14}{35}$

26. $\dfrac{3}{} = \dfrac{24}{32}$

27. $\dfrac{}{12} = \dfrac{8}{48}$

28. $\dfrac{7}{10} = \dfrac{49}{}$

29. $\dfrac{}{8} = \dfrac{45}{72}$

30. $\dfrac{}{12} = \dfrac{4}{48}$

31. $\dfrac{4}{9} = \dfrac{16}{}$

32. $\dfrac{2}{5} = \dfrac{}{50}$

Percentage

Percentage is a way of expressing a number as a fraction of 100. It is commonly used to represent proportions, rates, and comparisons. The symbol "%" is used to denote percentages.

To calculate a percentage, we multiply the given number by the appropriate fraction or decimal equivalent.

How to calculate a percentage:

Convert Percentage to Decimal: If the percentage is given as a percentage value (e.g., 25%), convert it to its decimal equivalent by dividing by 100.

$$\text{For example, 25\% as a decimal is } \frac{25}{100} = 0.25$$

Multiply: Multiply the decimal equivalent of the percentage by the given number. This gives us the portion of the number that represents the percentage.

$$100 \times 0.25 = 25\%$$

Result: The result is the calculated percentage value.

For example, to calculate 25% of 80:

Convert 25% to a decimal: 25% = 0.25.

Multiply 0.25 by 80: $0.25 \times 80 = 20$. The result is 20.

Percentage

Find the percentage of given numbers and percent values.

1. 200% of 300 = ☐

2. 30% of 200 = ☐

3. ☐ of 500 = 100

4. 25% of 500 = ☐

5. 5% of ☐ = 15

6. 7% of ☐ = 63

7. ☐ of 70 = 24.5

8. 300% of 800 = ☐

9. 40% of ☐ = 240

10. 90% of 300 = ☐

11. 15% of ⬚ = 6

12. 6% of 700 = ⬚

13. 9% of 800 = ⬚

14. ⬚ of 800 = 8

15. 70% of 900 = ⬚

16. ⬚ of 100 = 50

17. 7% of ⬚ = 5.6

18. 1% of ⬚ = 2

19. 100% of ⬚ = 500

20. 80% of ⬚ = 1.6

21. ⬚ of 500 = 20

22. 20% of ⬚ = 1

23. 3% of 600 = ☐

24. 90% of ☐ = 720

25. 50% of 80 = ☐

26. ☐ of 400 = 24

27. ☐ of 600 = 420

28. ☐ of 600 = 30

29. 60% of ☐ = 240

30. 8% of ☐ = 32

31. 30% of ☐ = 3

32. ☐ of 7 = 2.45

33. 40% of ☐ = 200

34. ☐ of 800 = 80

Convert Percent and Decimals

1. 0.85 =
____

2. 51 % =
____

3. 0.44 =
____

4. 68 % =
____

5. 0.21 =
____

6. 11 % =
____

7. 0.47 =
____

8. 0.25 =
____

9. 39 % =
____

10. 62 % =
____

11. 0.63 = _______________

12. 0.87 = _______________

13. 0.34 = _______________

14. 0.36 = _______________

15. 0.48 = _______________

16. 0.1 = _______________

17. 2 % = _______________

18. 0.64 = _______________

19. 100 % = _______________

20. 7 % = _______________

21. 0.15 = _______________

22. 18 % = _______________

23. 76 % = _______________

24. 94 % = _______________

25. 72 % = _______________

26. 14 % = _______________

27. 0.49 = _______________

28. 0.35 = _______________

29. 0.46 = _______________

30. 0.71 = _______________

31. 0.16 = _______________

32. 31 % = _______________

33. 0.75 = _______________

34. 41 % = _______________

<u>**Convert Fractions and Decimals**</u>

Fraction to Decimal

To transform a fraction into a decimal, we divide the numerator by the denominator.

For instance, $\frac{1}{4}$ equals 0.25 because when we divide 1 by 4, we get 0.25.

In certain cases, the resulting decimal repeats infinitely, like $\frac{1}{3}$, which equals 0.3333... In such instances, we round the decimal to a specific number of decimal places.

Decimal to Fraction

Step 1: Write down the decimal as a fraction with the decimal part in the numerator and the place value of the last digit in the denominator.

Step 2: Simplify the fraction if possible.

Convert: Ratio, Fraction, Percent, and Decimals

1.

	Ratio	Fraction	Percent	Decimal
a.		1/8		
b.			100%	
c.				0.889
d.			80%	
e.		11/14		
f.	2:3			
g.			50%	
h.			62.5%	
i.		1/4		
j.				0.45
k.				0.077
l.			60%	
m.	7:18			
n.	9:10			
o.			30%	

2.

	Ratio	Fraction	Percent	Decimal
a.	2:2			
b.			85.7%	
c.	6:16			
d.		2/15		
e.	17:19			
f.				0.556
g.		4/5		
h.		2/11		
i.		16/18		
j.			35.3%	
k.	15:17			
l.				0.25
m.			27.3%	
n.			25%	
o.			20%	

3.

	Ratio	Fraction	Percent	Decimal
a.			20%	
b.				0.308
c.			73.7%	
d.	15:17			
e.		2/14		
f.			27.3%	
g.				0.25
h.			5.9%	
i.				1
j.				0.579
k.	6:12			
l.			12.5%	
m.				0.857
n.			33.3%	
o.				0.941

<u>**Area and Perimeter**</u>

The area of a shape represents the amount of space it occupies. The perimeter of a shape is the total distance around its outer edge.

Area of Rectangle

For a square, since all four sides are equal, we only need to know the length of one side to find its area. We can calculate the area of a square by multiplying the length of one side by itself (squared). So, if the length of one side of the square is 's', then the area (A) is given by:

A = s x s

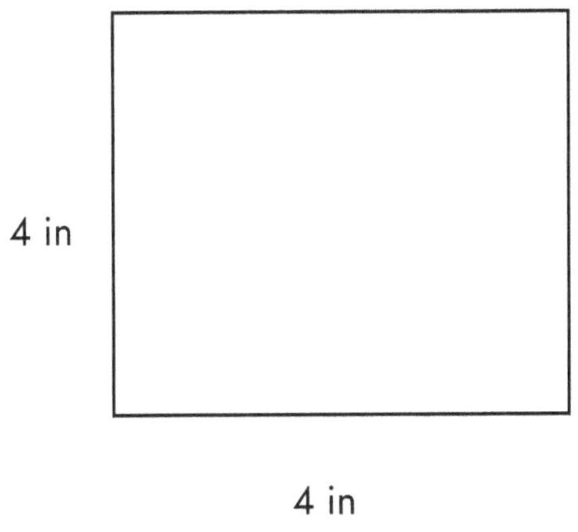

4 in

4 in

A = 4 x 4

A = 16

Perimeter of Rectangle

For a square, since all four sides are equal, we can find the perimeter by adding up the lengths of all four sides. If 's' represents the length of one side, then the perimeter (P) is given by:

$$P = 4 \times s$$

$$P = 4 \times 4$$

$$P = 16$$

Area of Triangle:

The area of a triangle represents the amount of space enclosed within its three sides. The formula for calculating the area of a triangle depends on the type of triangle. For a general triangle, we use the formula:

$$A = \frac{1}{2} \times base \times height$$

Where:

- A represents the area of the triangle.

- The base is the length of any one side of the triangle.

- The height is the perpendicular distance from the base to the opposite vertex.

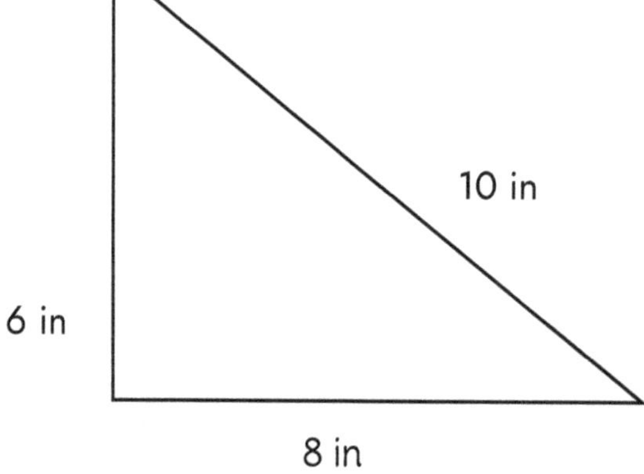

$$A = \frac{1}{2} \times \text{base} \times \text{height}$$

$$A = \frac{1}{2} \times 6 \times 8$$

$$A = \frac{1}{2} \times 48$$

$$A = 24$$

Perimeter of Triangle:

The perimeter of a triangle is the total length of its three sides. To find the perimeter, we simply add the lengths of all three sides together:

$$P = \text{side1} + \text{side2} + \text{side3}$$

$$P = 6 + 8 + 10$$

$$P = 24$$

Equilateral Triangle

An equilateral triangle is a triangle in which all three sides are equal in length. To find the area and perimeter of an equilateral triangle, we can use the following formulas:

- Area (A): $\frac{\sqrt{3}}{4} \times a^2$ where a is the length of one side of the equilateral triangle.
- Perimeter (P): $P = 3a$ where a is the length of one side of the equilateral triangle.

Let's solve a problem:

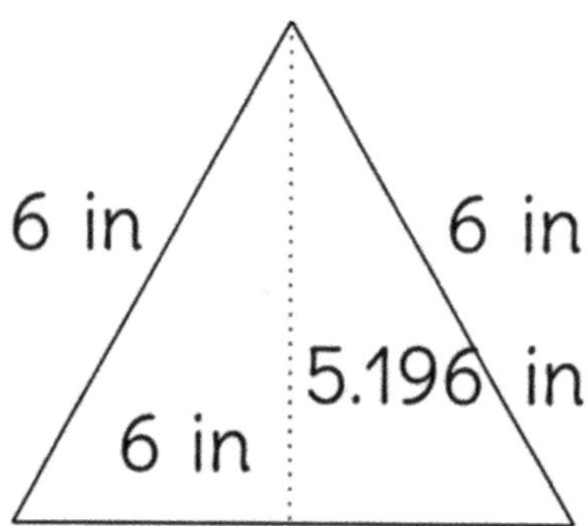

Area of Equilateral Triangle:

$$\text{Area (A): } \frac{\sqrt{3}}{4} \times (6)^2$$

$$\text{Area (A): } \frac{\sqrt{3}}{4} \times 36$$

$$\text{Area (A): } \frac{36\sqrt{3}}{4}$$

$$\text{Area (A): } \frac{36(1.73)}{4}$$

$$\text{Area (A): } \frac{62.35}{4}$$

$$\text{Area (A): } 15.59 \text{ in}^2$$

Perimeter of Equilateral Triangle:

$$P = 3a$$

$$P = 3(6) = 18$$

Isosceles Triangle

An isosceles triangle is a triangle with at least two sides of equal length. The angles opposite the equal sides are also equal.

Area of Isosceles Triangle

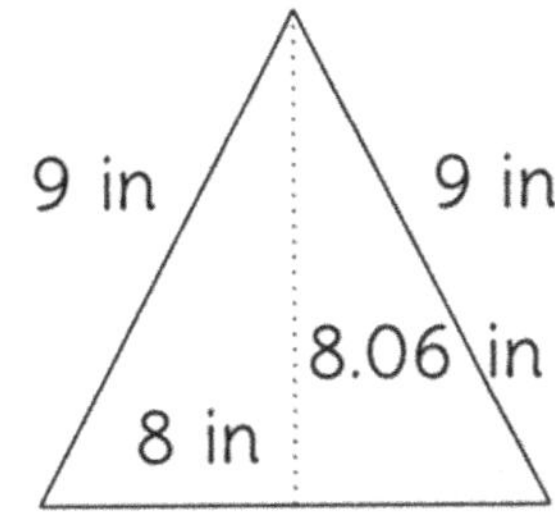

$$A = \frac{1}{2} \times \text{base} \times \text{height}$$

$$A = \frac{1}{2} \times 8 \times 8$$

$$A = \frac{1}{2} \times 64$$

$$A = 32$$

Perimeter of Isosceles Triangle

The perimeter of a triangle is the total length of its three sides. To find the perimeter, we simply add the lengths of all three sides together:

$$P = \text{side1} + \text{side2} + \text{side3}$$

$$P = 9 + 9 + 8$$

$$P = 26$$

Scalene Triangle

A scalene triangle is a triangle with no equal sides and no equal angles. The formula for finding various properties of a scalene triangle is as follows:

Area (A): The area of a scalene triangle can be calculated using Heron's fo rmula, which is given by:

$$A = \sqrt{s(s-a)(s-b)(s-c)}$$

where s is the semi-perimeter of the triangle,

and a, b, and c are the lengths of its three sides.

Perimeter (P): The perimeter of a scalene triangle is the sum of the lengths of its three sides.

$$P = side1 + side2 + side3$$

Let's find the Area and Perimeter of a Scalene Triangle:

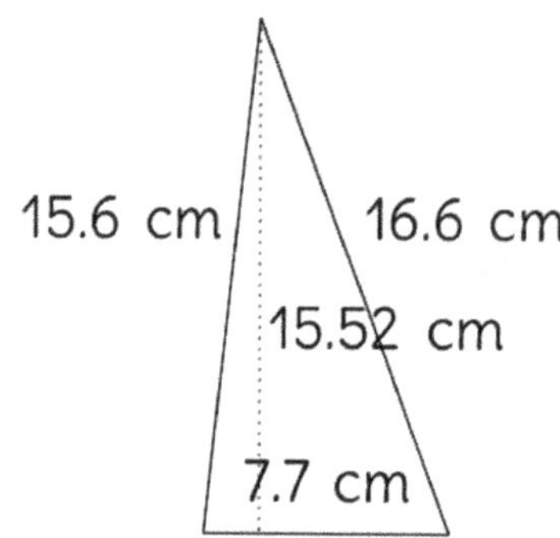

Area (A): First, we calculate the semi-perimeter (s):

$$S = \frac{a+b+c}{2} = \frac{15.6 + 16.6 + 7.7}{2} = \frac{39.8}{2} = 19.9 \text{ cm}$$

Heron's formula to find the area:

$$A = \sqrt{s(s-a)(s-b)(s-c)}$$

$$A = \sqrt{19.9\,(19.9-15.6)\,(19.9-16.6)\,(19.9-7.7)}$$

$$A = \sqrt{19.9 \times 4.3 \times 3.3 \times 12.2}$$

$$A = \sqrt{3445} \approx 59$$

Perimeter (P):

$$P = side1 + side2 + side3$$

$$P = 15.6 + 16.6 + 7.7$$

$$P = 39.8$$

Area and Perimeter of an L-shape

The L-shaped figure typically consists of two rectangles joined together to form an L-shape. To find the area and perimeter of an L-shaped figure, we will need to calculate the areas and perimeters of each rectangle and then combine them.

Area=Area of Rectangle 1 + Area of Rectangle 2

Perimeter=Perimeter of Rectangle 1 + Perimeter of Rectangle 2

Let's find the Area and Perimeter of an L-shape:

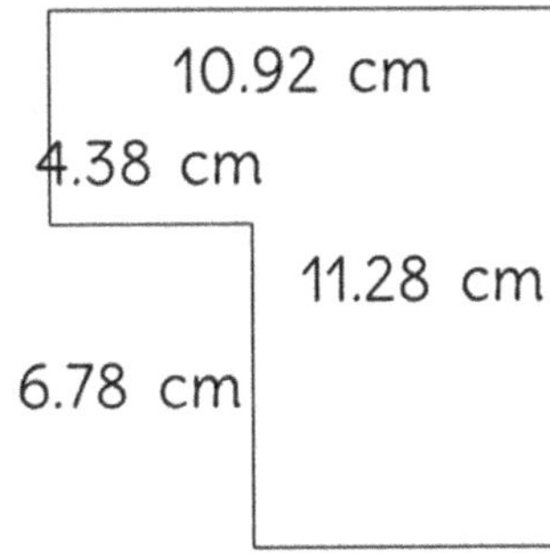

Area of L-Shape

$$\text{Area 1} = 4.38 \times 4.5 = 19.7 \text{ cm}^2$$

$$\text{Area 2} = 11.28 \times 6.54 = 73.7 \text{ cm}^2$$

$$\text{Area} = 19.7 + 73.7$$

$$\text{Area} = 93.481 \text{ cm}^2$$

Perimeter of L-Shape

$$P = 11.28 + 6.54 + 6.78 + 4.38 + 4.5 + 10.92$$

$$P = 44.4 \text{ cm}$$

Area and Perimeter of U-shape

U-shape is basically composed of three rectangles, we'll need to calculate the area and perimeter of each rectangle separately and then sum them up.

Area of the U-shape:

The total area (A) of the U-shape is the sum of the areas of the three rectangles:

$$A = A1 + A2 + A3$$

Perimeter of the U-shape: The total perimeter (P) of the U-shape is the sum of the perimeters of the three rectangles:

$$P = P1 + P2 + P3$$

Let's find the area and perimeter of the following U-shape:

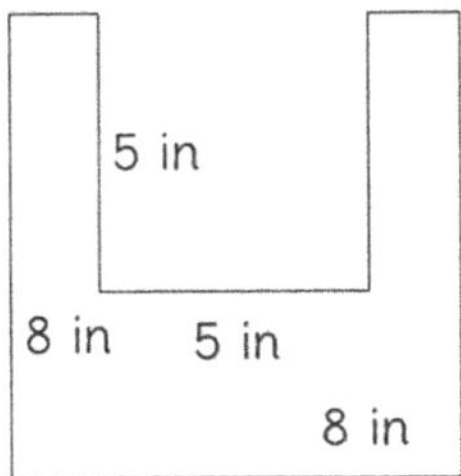

Area:

$$A1 = 8 \times 1.5 = 12 + A2 = 3 \times 5 = 15 + A3 = 8 \times 1.5 = 12$$

$$= 12 + 15 + 12$$

$$= 39 \text{ in}^2$$

Perimeter:

$$2 \times 8 + 2 \times 5 + 2 \times 8$$

$$= 16 + 10 + 16$$

$$= 42$$

Area and Perimeter of T-shape

The T-shape consists of two rectangles joined together to form a T-like structure.

Area of the T-shape:

To find the total area of the T-shape, we need to calculate the areas of both rectangles and then add them together.

$$\text{Area of Rectangle 1} = \text{Length} \times \text{Width}$$

$$\text{Area of Rectangle 2} = \text{Length} \times \text{Width}$$

$$\text{Total Area} = \text{Area of Rectangle 1} + \text{Area of Rectangle 2}$$

The perimeter of the T-shape is the sum of the perimeters of the two rectangles, minus the length of the overlapping side:

$$\text{Perimeter} = 2(l1+w1) + 2(l2+w2) - (w1\text{-}w2)$$

Area= 12 × 13 + 6 × 4

Area= 156 + 24

Area= 180 in²

Perimeter= 2(12+13) +2(6+4) − (12-4)

Perimeter=2(25) + 2(10) − 8

Perimeter= 50 + 20 − 8

Perimeter= 62 in²

Area and Perimeter of Parallelogram

A parallelogram is a four-sided polygon with opposite sides that are parallel and equal in length. To find the area and perimeter of a parallelogram, we use specific formulas based on its dimensions.

For example:

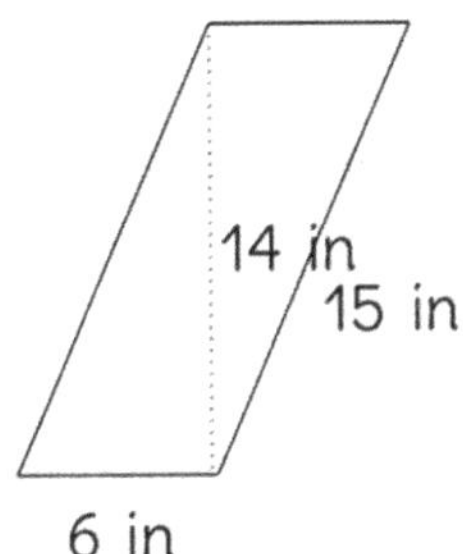

Let's denote:

- The length of one side of the parallelogram as $a = 15$.

- The length of an adjacent side (parallel to a) $b = 6$.

- The height of the parallelogram (perpendicular distance between the two parallel sides) as $h=14$

Area of Parallelogram

$$\text{Area} = \text{Base} \times \text{Height}$$

$$\text{Area} = 6 \times 1\ 4$$

$$\text{Area} = 84$$

Perimeter of Parallelogram

$$2(a + b)$$

$$= 2(15+6)$$

$$= 2(21)$$

$$= 42$$

Area and Perimeter of Trapezoids

A trapezoid is a quadrilateral with at least one pair of parallel sides. To find the area and perimeter of a trapezoid, we use specific formulas based on its dimensions.

For example:

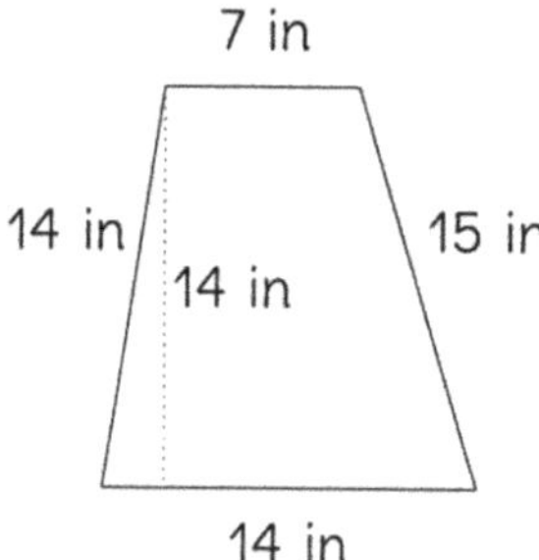

Let's denote:

- The lengths of the parallel sides of the trapezoid as $a = 7$ and $b = 14$.

- The lengths of the non-parallel sides as $c = 14$ and $d = 15$.

- The height of the trapezoid (the perpendicular distance between the parallel sides) as $h=14$.

Area of the Trapezoid:

The area of a trapezoid is given by the formula:

$$\text{Area} = \frac{1}{2} \times \text{Height} \times (\text{Sum of the lengths of the parallel sides})$$

$$\text{Area} = \frac{1}{2} \times h \times (a + b)$$

$$\text{Area} = \frac{1}{2} \times 14 \times (7 + 14)$$

$$\text{Area} = \frac{1}{2} \times 14 \times 21$$

Area= 147 in^2

Perimeter of the Trapezoid:

Perimeter= 7 + 14 + 14 + 15

=50 in^2

Area and Perimeter

1.

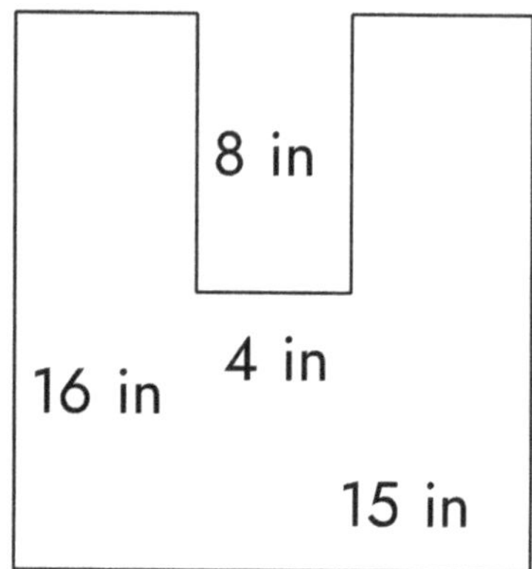

2.

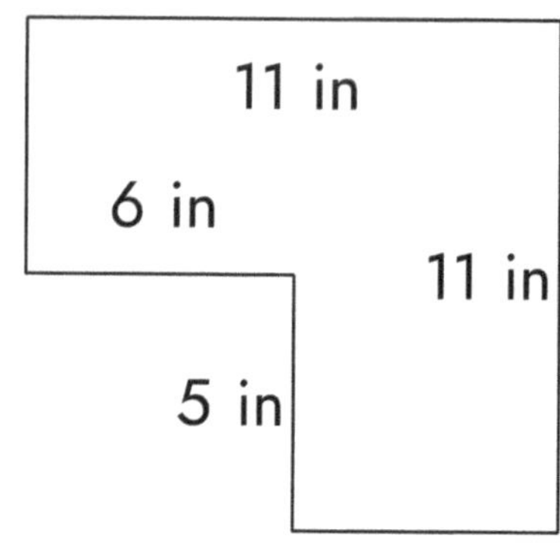

3.

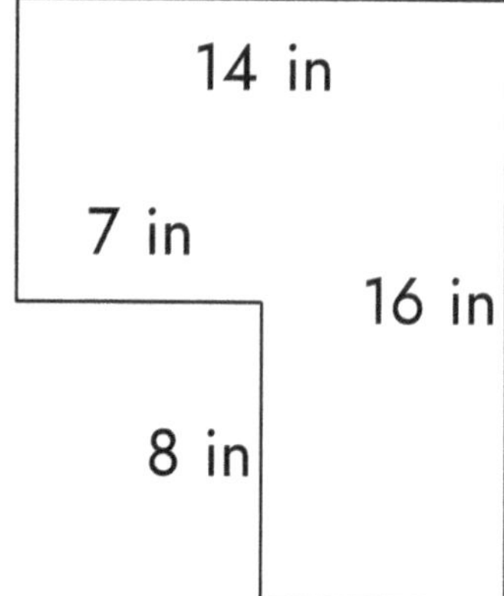

4.

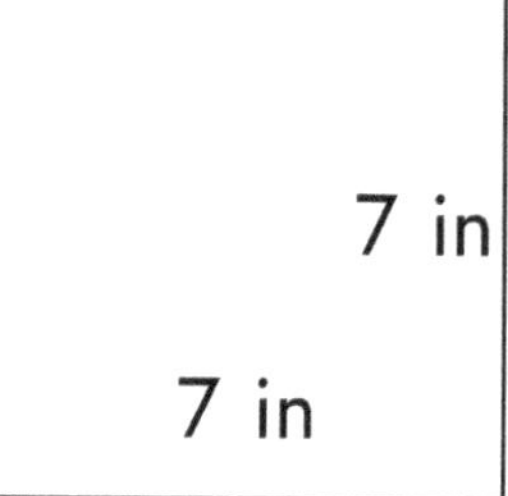

SUMMER MATH WORKBOOK
NAME:
BUILDING ACTIVITIES

5.

10 in
10 in
8.66 in
10 in

6.

16 in
16 in
14.62 in
13 in

7.

14 in
7 in
16 12 in
16 in

8.

6 in
15 in
5 in
17 in

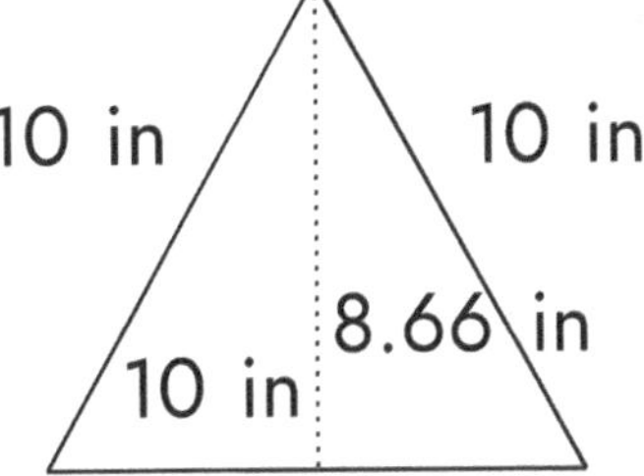

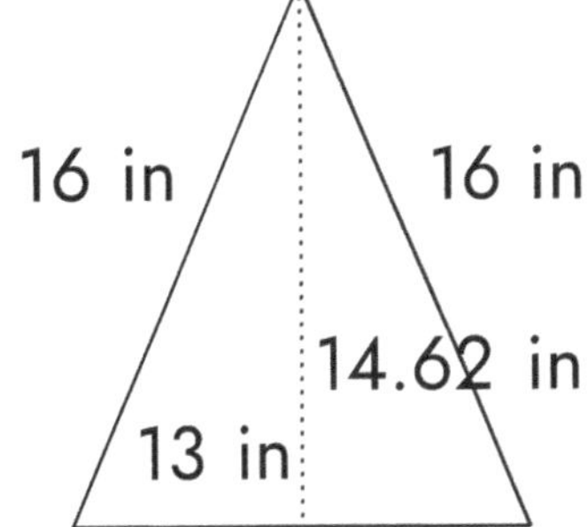

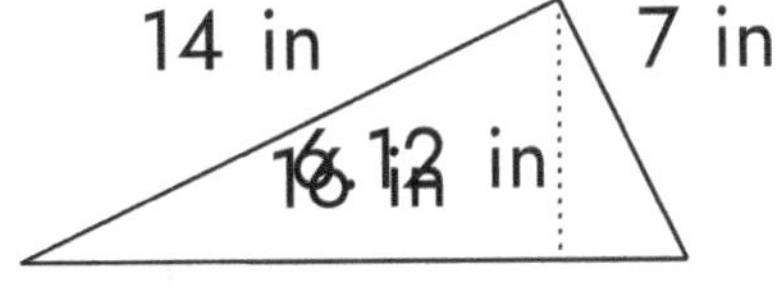

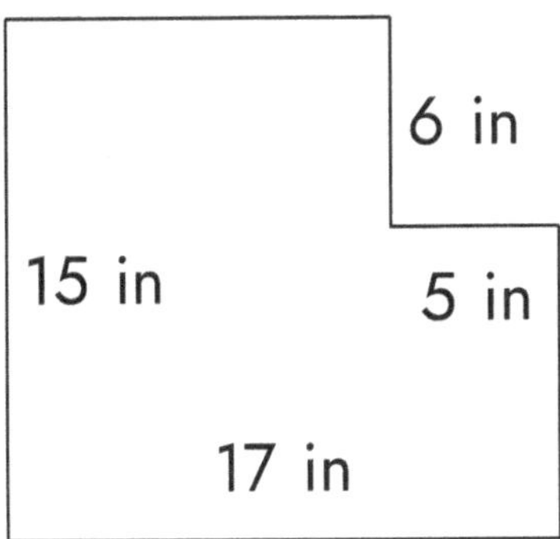

9.

8 in
14 in
8 in
13 in

10.

18 in
12 in
13 in

11.

18 in
13 in
12 in

12.

6 in
6 in
6 in
5.196 in

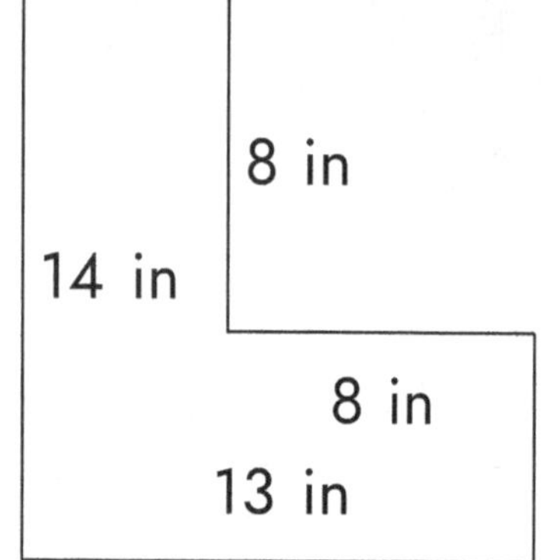

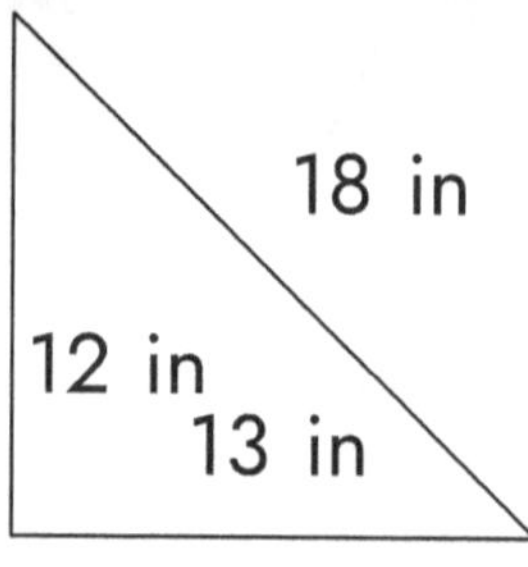

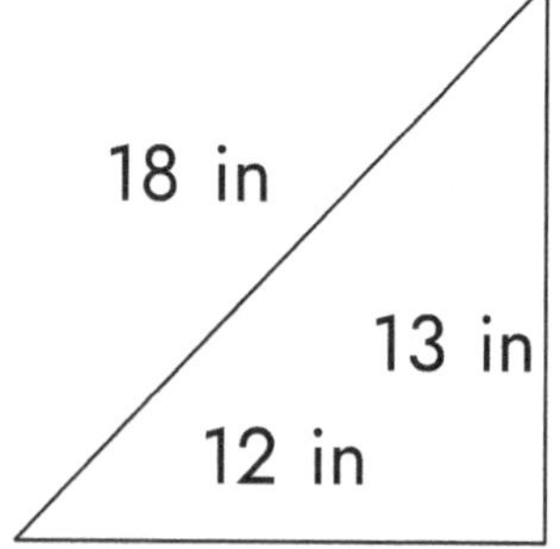

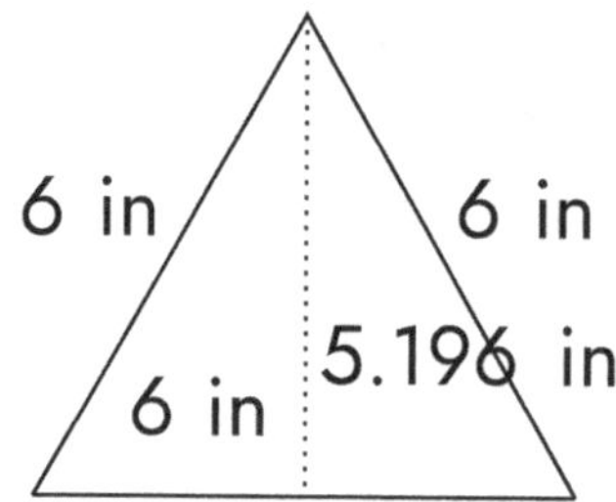

13.

7 in
4 in
10 in
5 in

14.

6 in
5 in

15.

13 in
13 in
12.60 in
4 in

16.

11 in
6 in
5.40 in
12 in

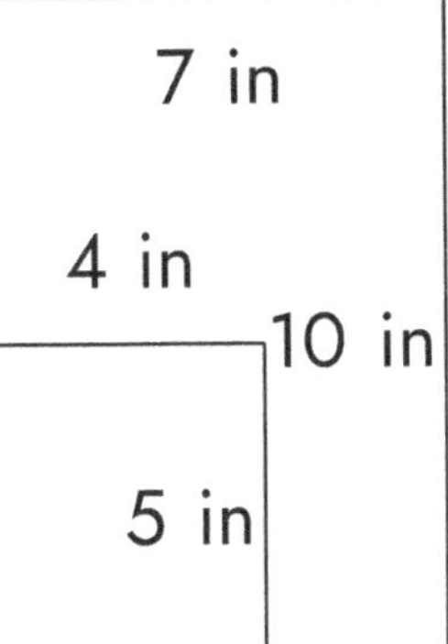

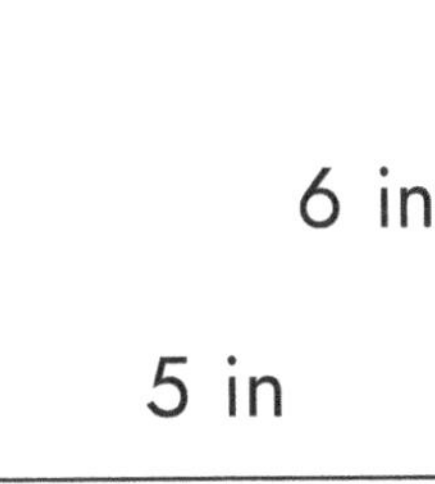

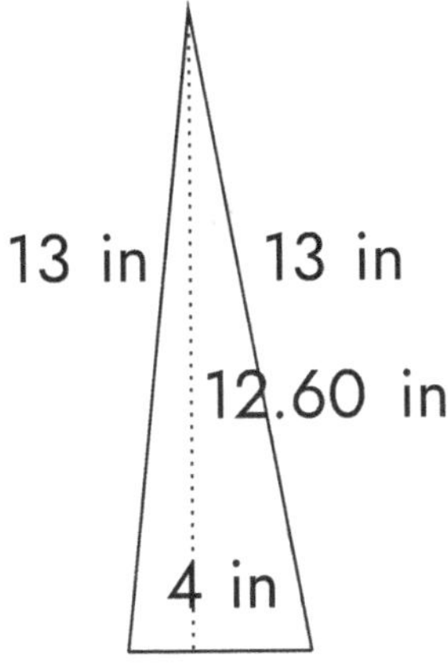

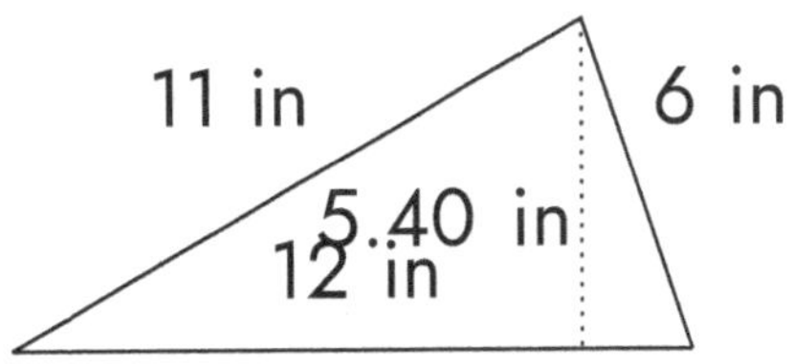

17.

12 in

13 in

18.

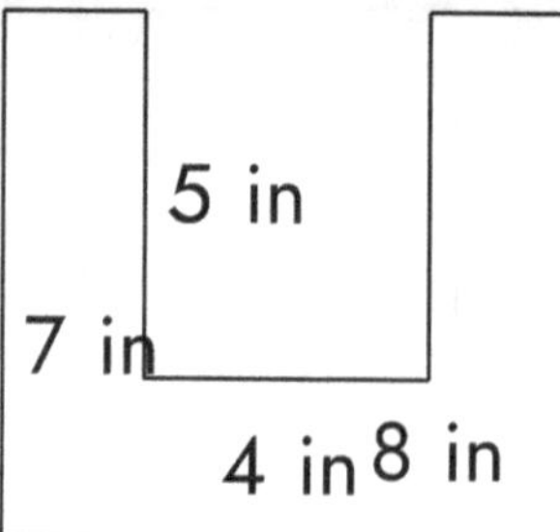

19.

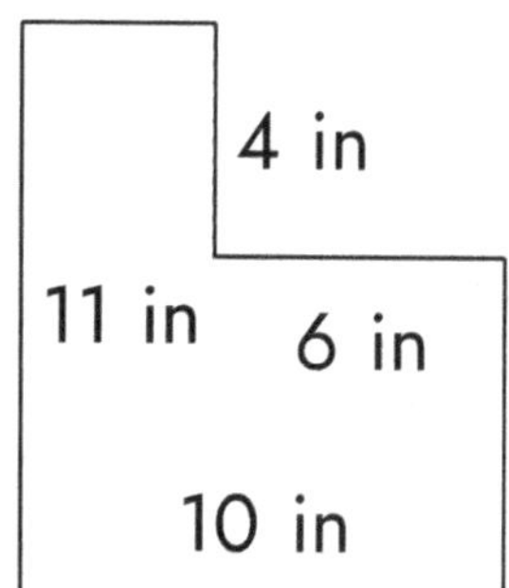

20.

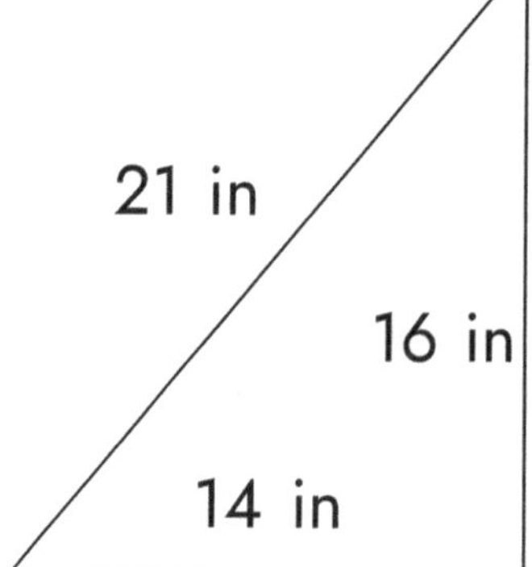

21.

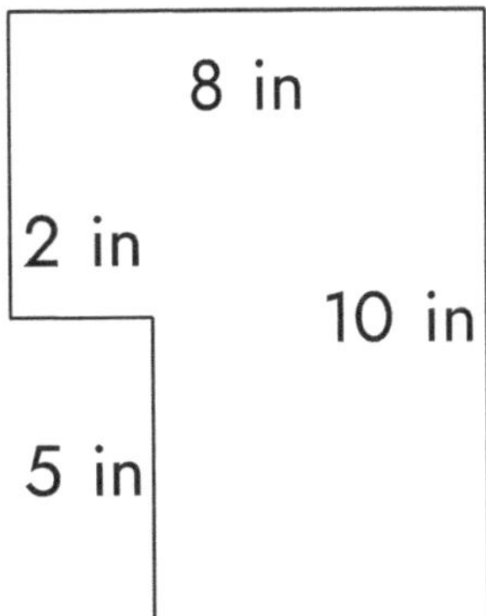

22.

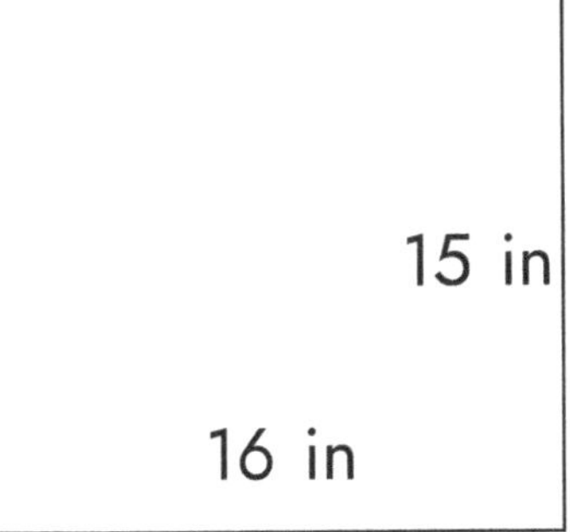

23.

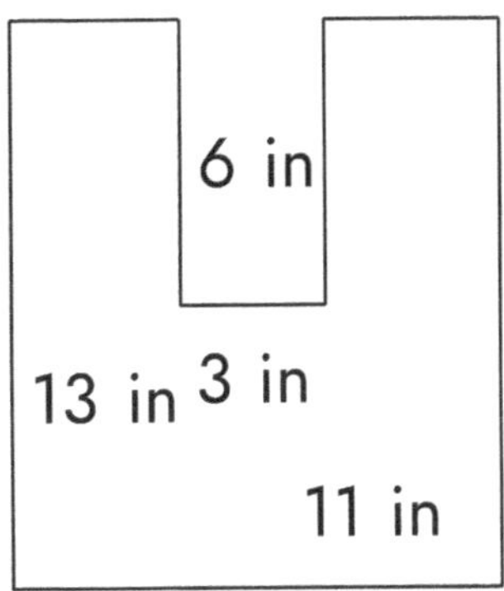

24.

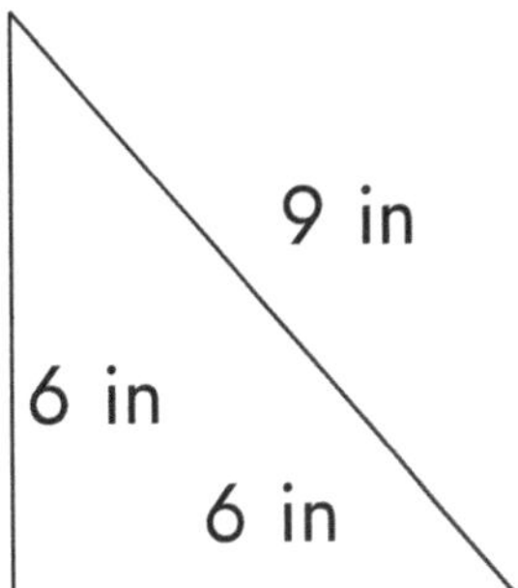

25.

5 in

6 in

26. 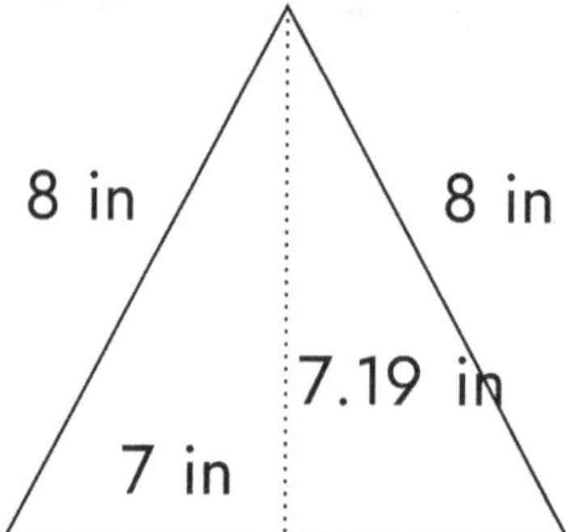

27. 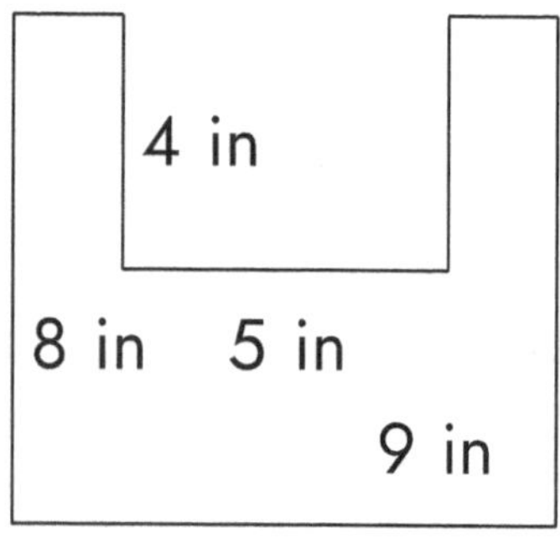

28. 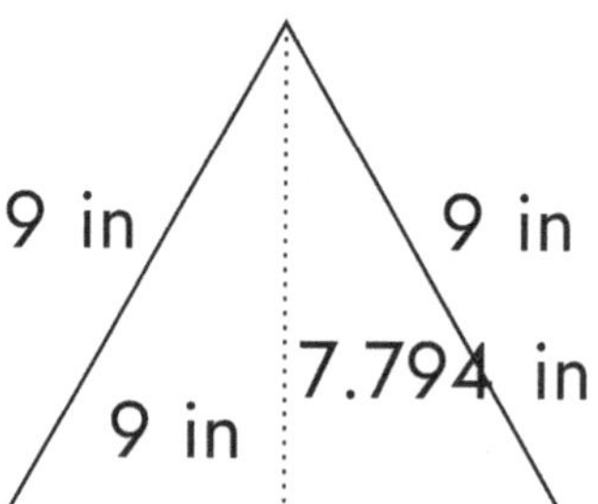

Angles

Types of Angles: Angles can be classified based on their measures:

- **Acute Angle:** An angle less than 90°.

- **Right Angle:** An angle exactly equal to 90°.

- **Obtuse Angle:** An angle greater than 90° and less than 180°.

- **Straight Angle:** An angle exactly equal to 180°.

- **Reflex Angle:** An angle greater than 180° and less than 360°.

- **Full Angle:** An angle equal to 360°.

Measure angles with a protractor. It looks like a semicircle or a half-disc with degree markings from 0° to 180°. To measure an angle using a protractor, we place the center of the protractor at the vertex of the angle, align one side of the angle with the zero mark on the protractor, and read the degree measure where the other side intersects the protractor.

For example, let's measure the following angle.

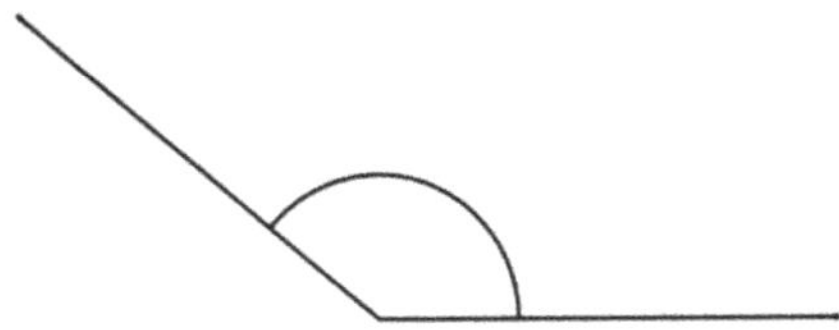

The angle is 140°.

We also know that the angle is greater than 90° and less than 180°, so this is an Obtuse angle.

Classify and Measure Angles

1.

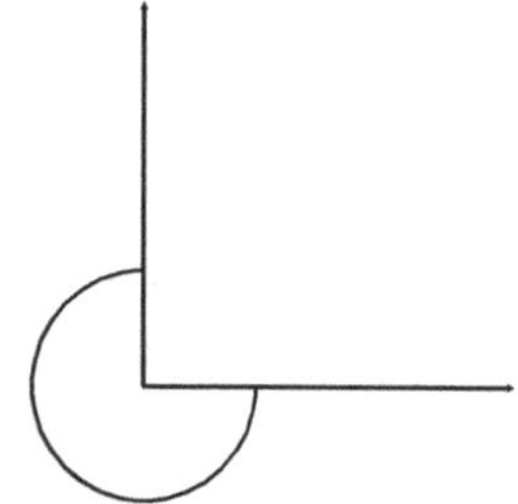

____

2.

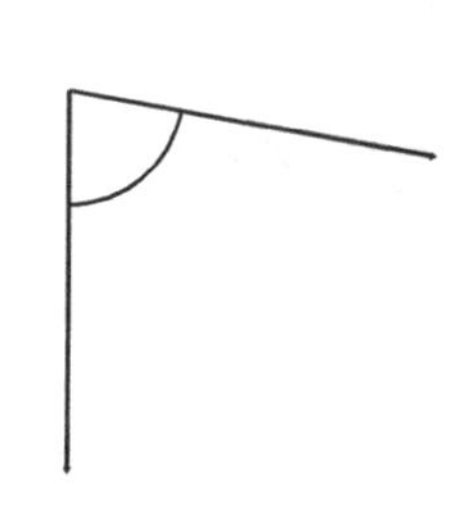

____

3.

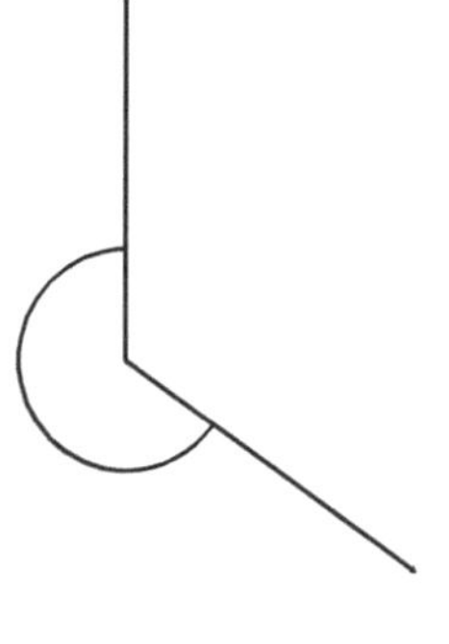

____

4.

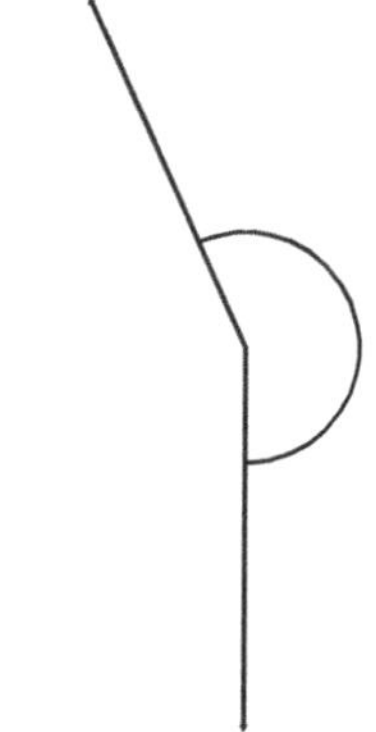

____

5.

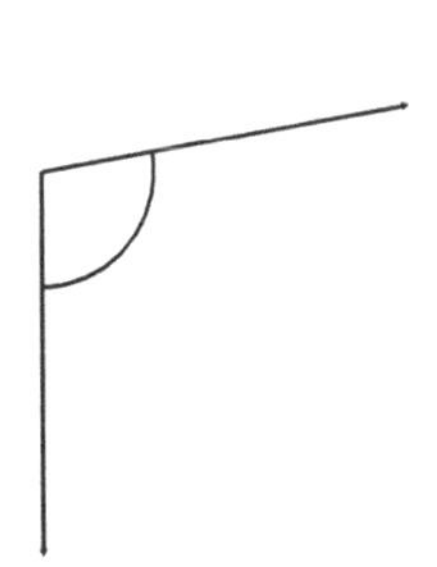

6.

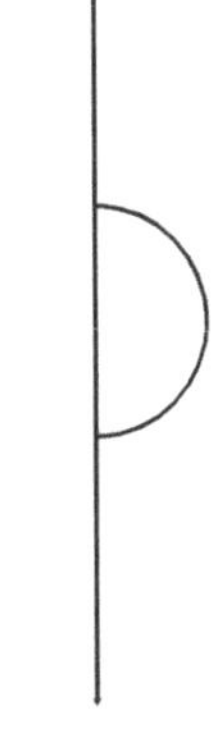

7.

8.

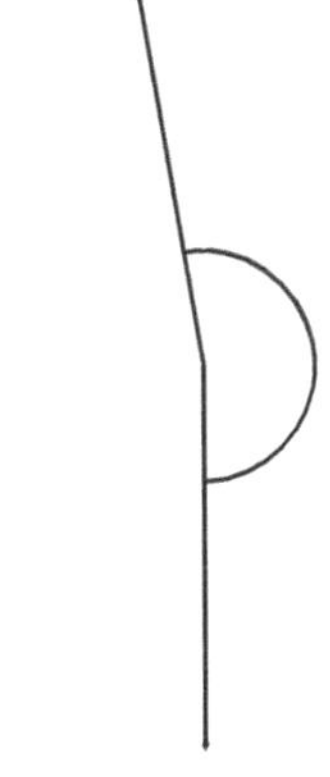

9.

____

10.

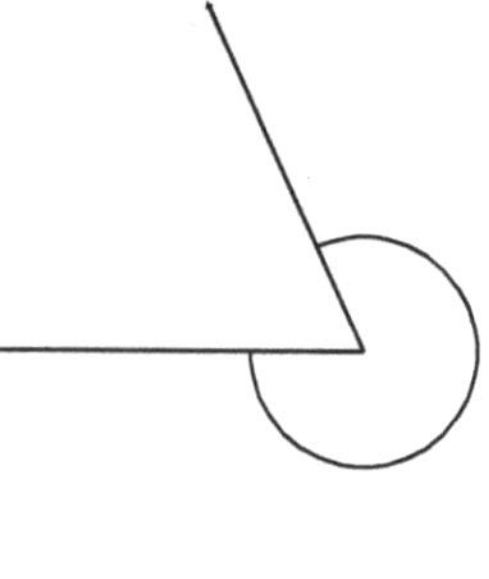

____

11.

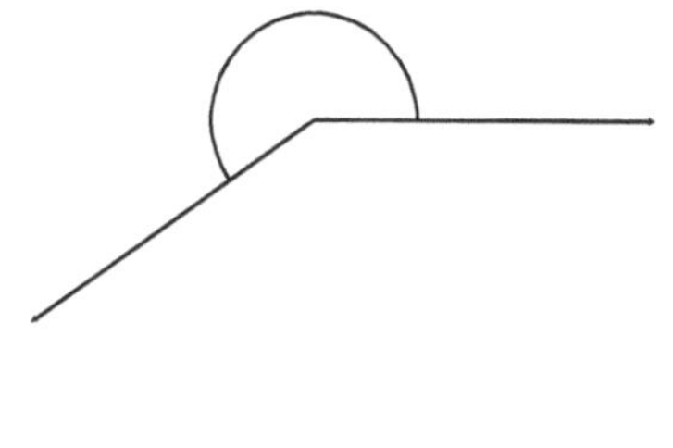

____

12.

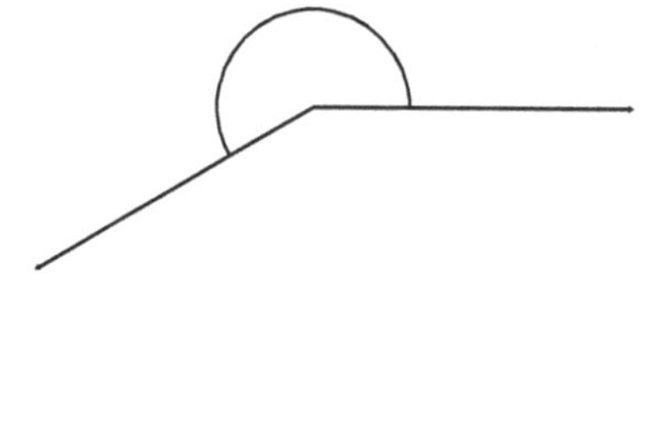

____

13.

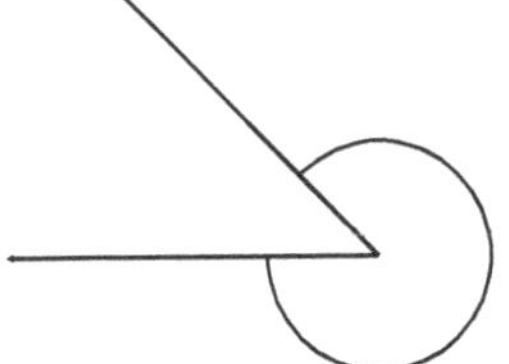

____

14.

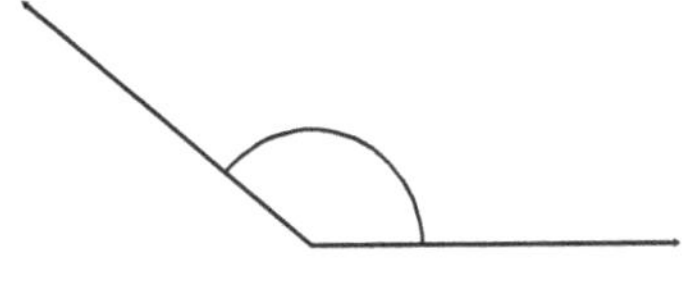

____

15.

____

16.

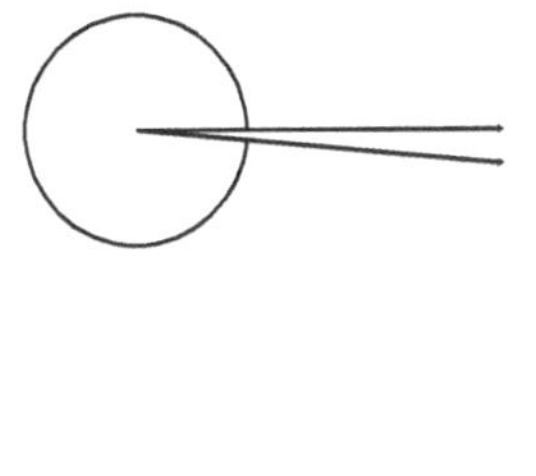

____

17.

18.

19.

20.

21.

22.

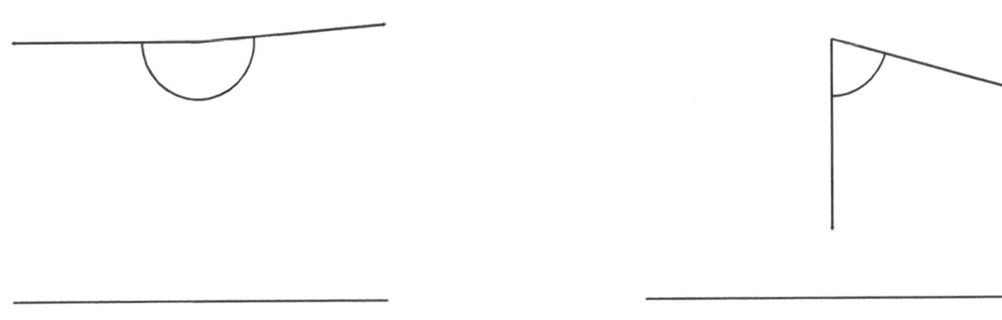

23.

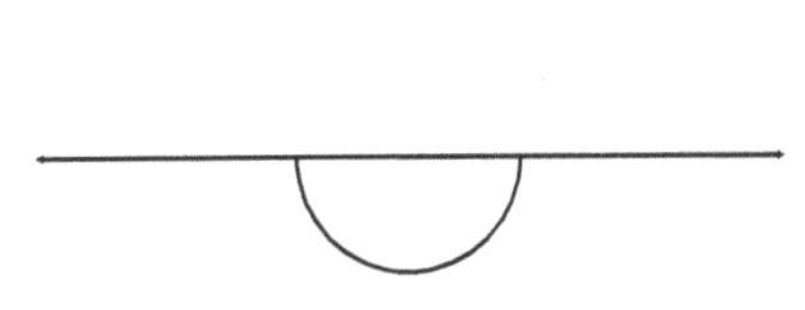

24.

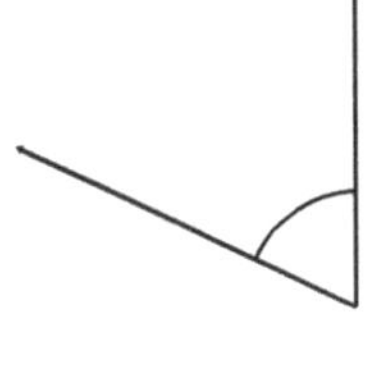

Volume and surface Area

Volume refers to the amount of space occupied by a three-dimensional object. For shapes like cubes or rectangular prisms, we calculate volume by multiplying their length, width, and height.

To find the volume V of a rectangular prism, we use the formula:

$$Volume \ = \ length \ x \ width \ x \ height$$

Surface Area represents the total area covering all the faces of a three-dimensional object. For shapes like cubes or rectangular prisms, we find the surface area by summing the areas of all its faces.

The formula for surface area SA of a cube or rectangular prism is:

$$Surface \ Area \ = \ 2lw \ + \ 2lh \ + \ 2wh$$

Where: l is the length, w is the width, and h is the height of the object.

For example: Let's find the Volume and Surface Area of following rectangular prisms:

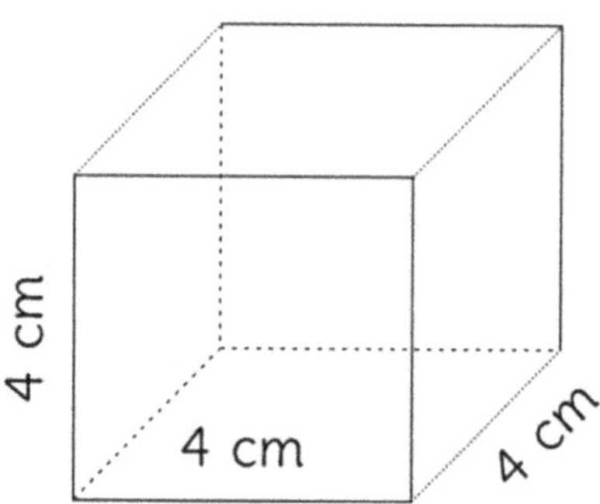

$$Volume \ = \ length \ \times \ width \ \times \ height$$

$$= 4 \times 4 \times 4$$

$$= 64 \text{ cm}^2$$

$$Surface\ Area\ =\ 2lw\ +\ 2lh\ +\ 2wh$$

$$= 2(4 \times 4) + 2(4 \times 4) + 2(4 \times 4)$$

$$= 32 + 32 + 32$$

$$= 96 \text{ cm2}$$

Different 3D objects have unique formulas for finding their volume and surface area. Here are some common ones:

1. Cube:

- Volume: $V = s^3$ (where s is the length of one side of the cube)

- Surface area: $SA = 6s^2$

2. Sphere:

- Volume: $V = \left(\frac{4}{3}\right)\pi r^3$ (where r is the radius of the sphere)

- Surface area: $SA = 4\pi r^2$

3. Cone:

- Volume: $V = \left(\frac{1}{3}\right)\pi r^2 h$ (where r is the radius of the base and h is the height of the cone)

- Surface area: $SA = \pi r^2 + \pi r \sqrt{(r^2 + h^2)}$

4. Cylinder:

- Volume: $V = \pi r^2 h$ (where r is the radius of the base and h is the height of the cylinder)

- Surface area: $SA = 2\pi r^2 + 2\pi rh$

5. Pyramid:

- Volume: $V = (\frac{1}{3})Bh$ (where B is the area of the base and h is the height of the pyramid)

- Surface area: $SA = B + \frac{1}{2}Pl$ (where P is the perimeter of the base and l is the slant height of the pyramid)

Volume and Surface Area

1. 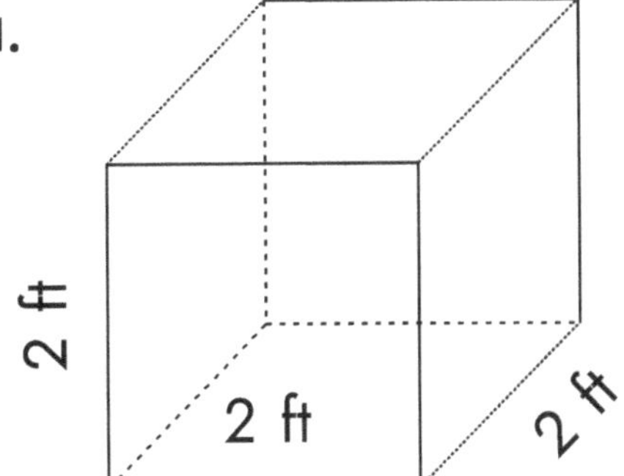

2. 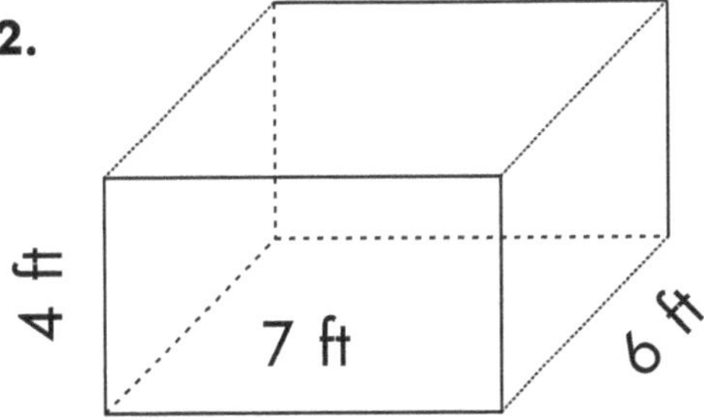

3. 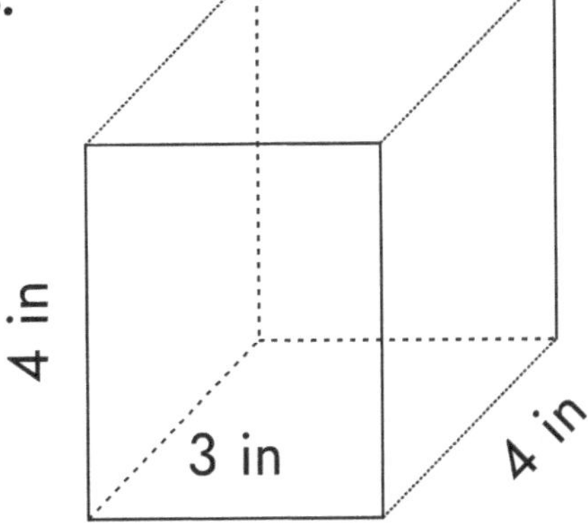

4. 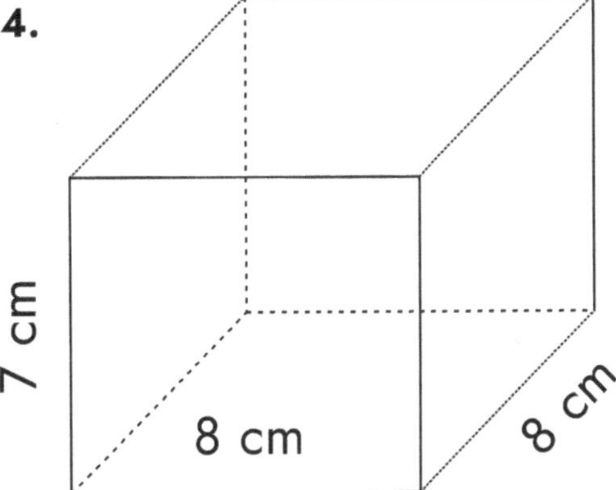

SUMMER MATH WORKBOOK
NAME:
BUILDING ACTIVITIES

5.

6 ft
6 ft
6 ft

6.

5 in
6 in
5 in

7.

9 in
6 in
6 in

8.

7 in
9 in
11 in

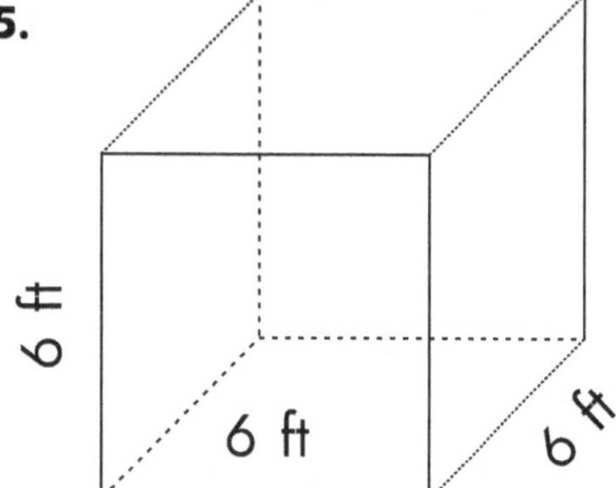

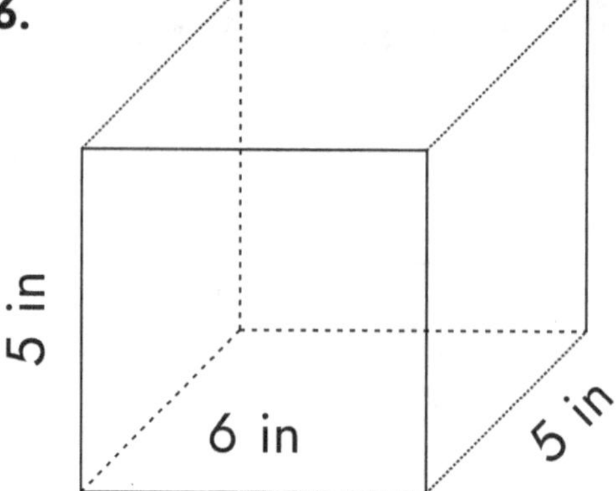

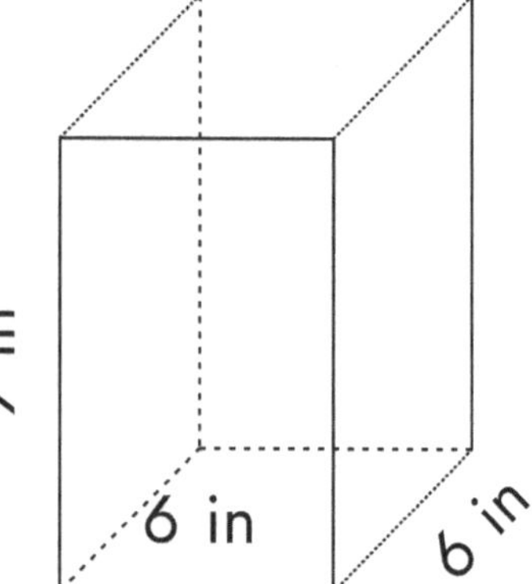

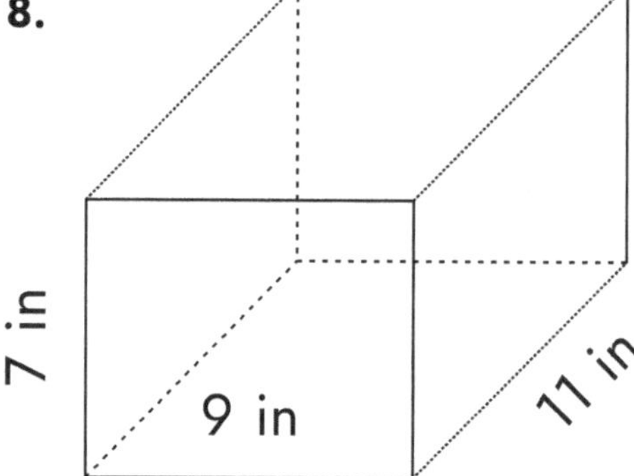

SUMMER MATH
WORKBOOK
BUILDING ACTIVITIES

9.

6 in
7 in
6 in

10.

7 cm
10 cm
8 cm

11.

4 cm
6 cm

12.

3 ft
2 ft
3 ft

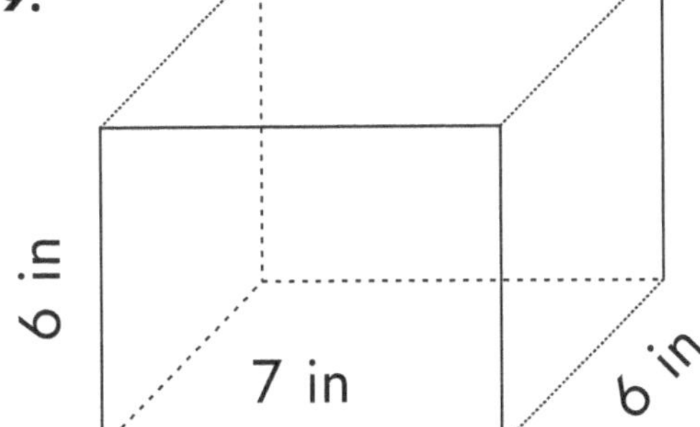

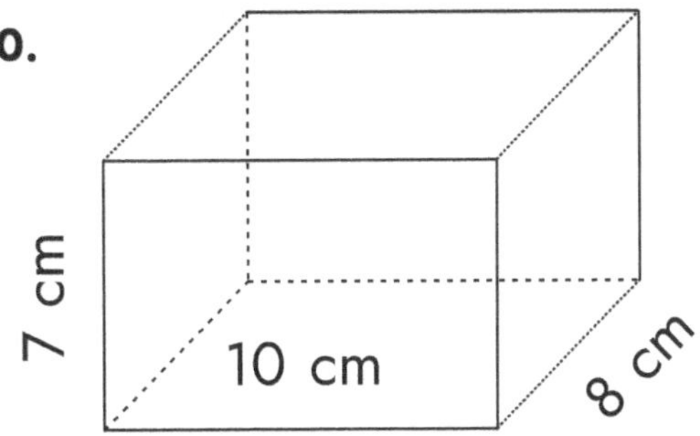

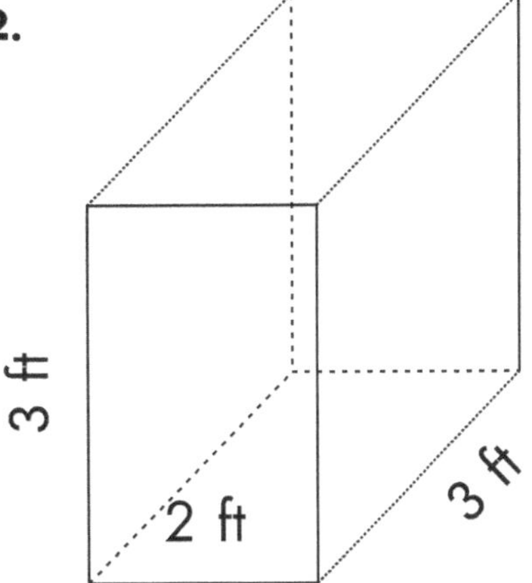

13.

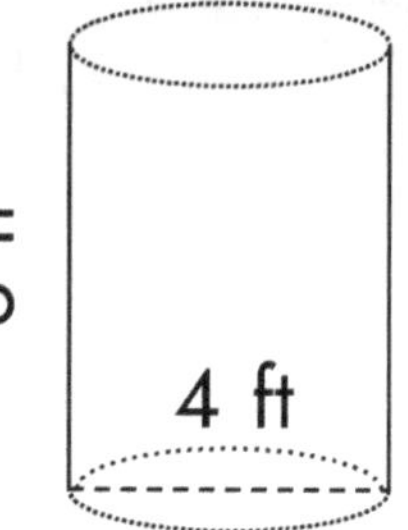

14.

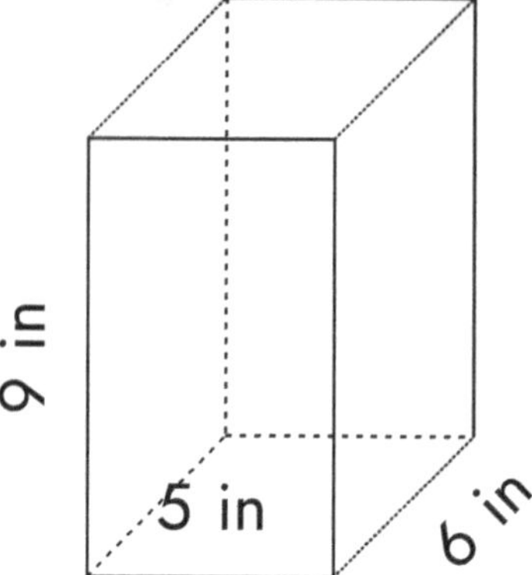

15.

16.

17.

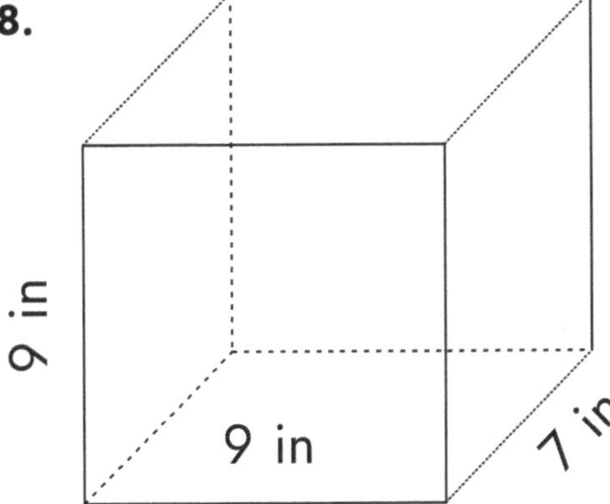

18.

19.

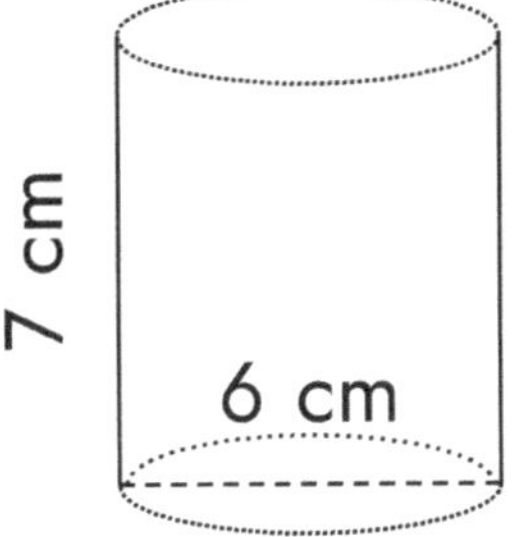

20.

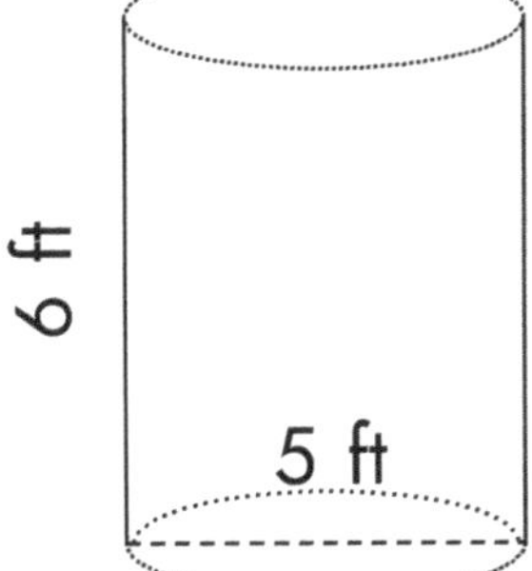

SUMMER MATH WORKBOOK
NAME:
BUILDING ACTIVITIES

21.

9 ft
11 ft

22.

6 ft
6 ft
10 ft

23.

7 cm
6 cm
6 cm

24.

3 ft
3 ft
2 ft

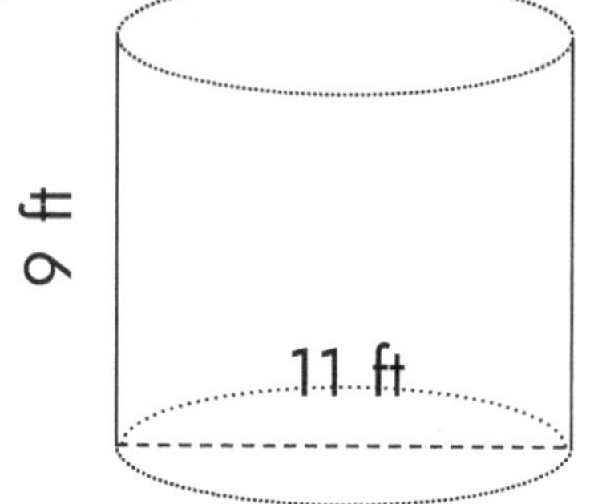

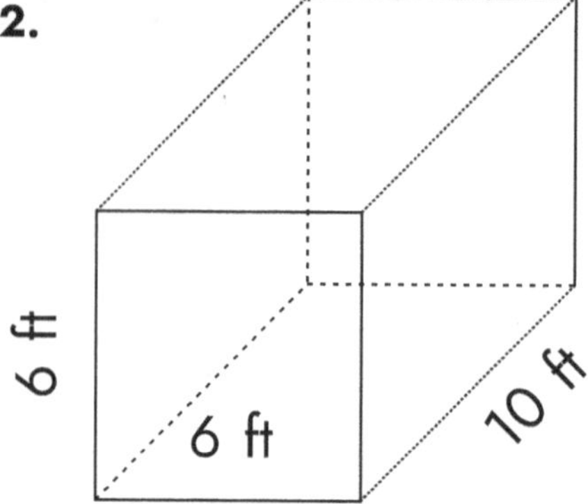

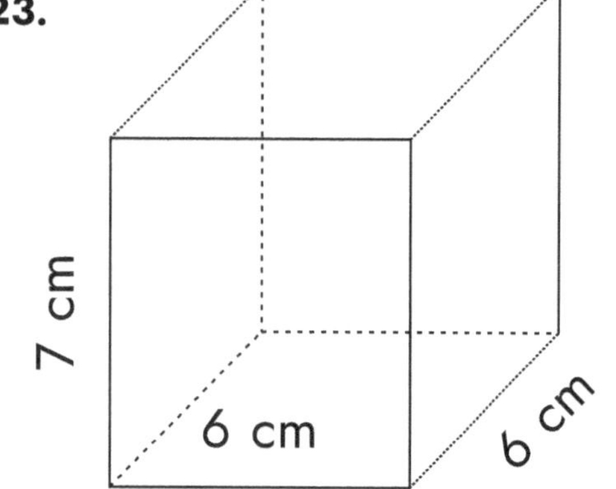

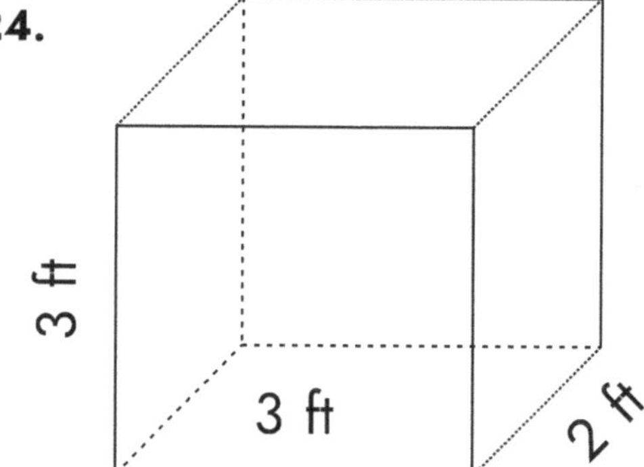

25.

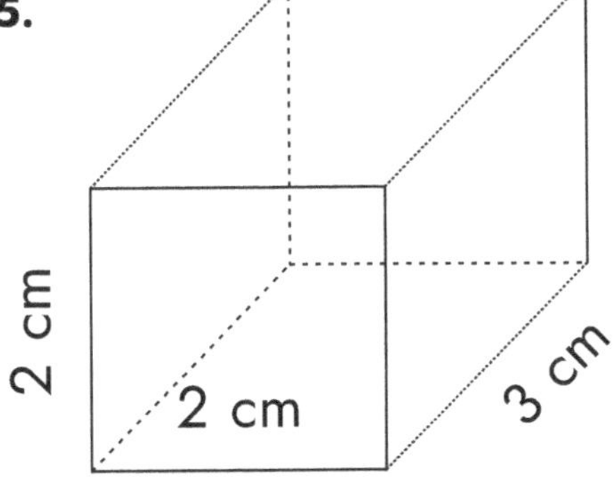

26.

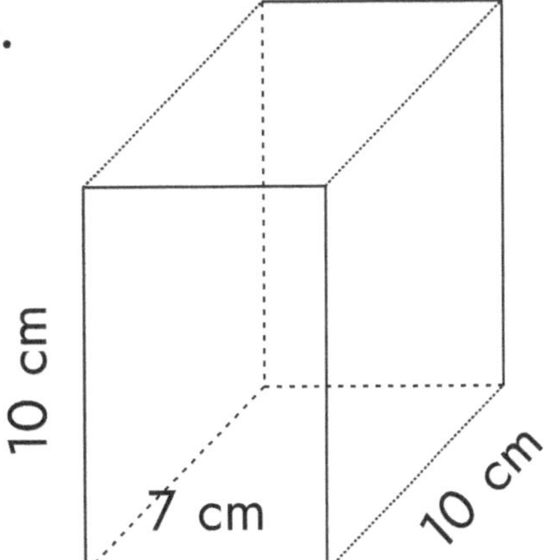

27.

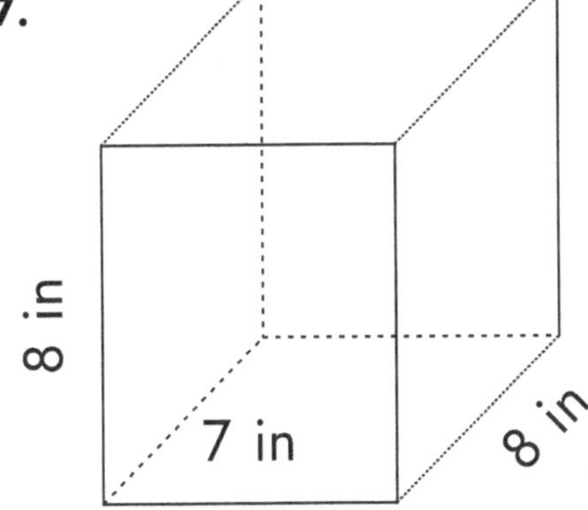

28.

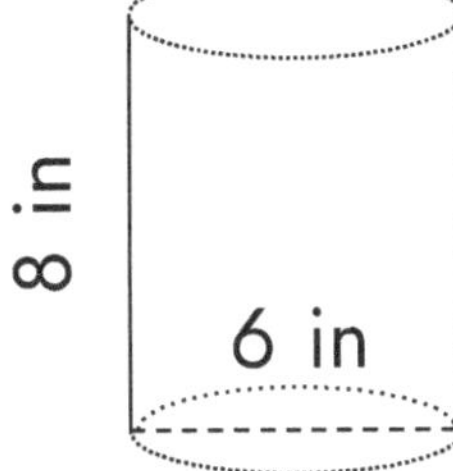

SUMMER MATH WORKBOOK
NAME:
BUILDING ACTIVITIES

29.

3 in
4 in
4 in

30.

8 ft
9 ft

31.

6 in
5 in
8 in

32.

4 cm
4 cm
3 cm

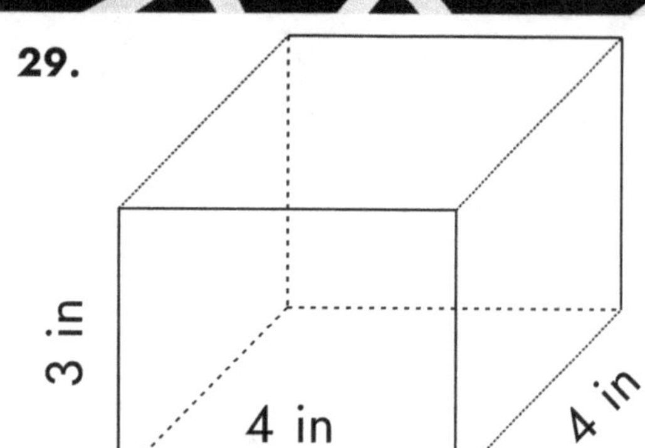

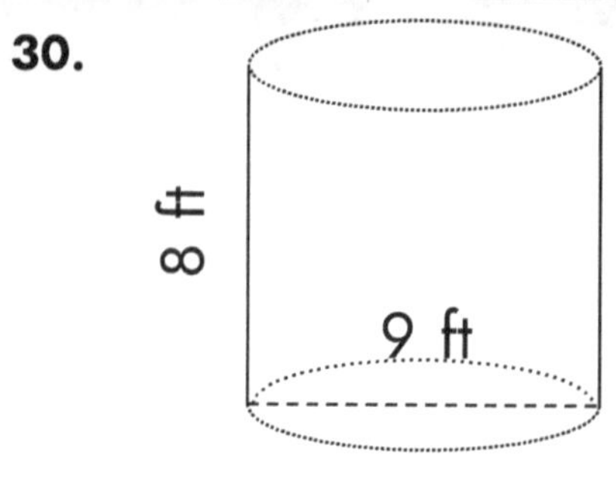

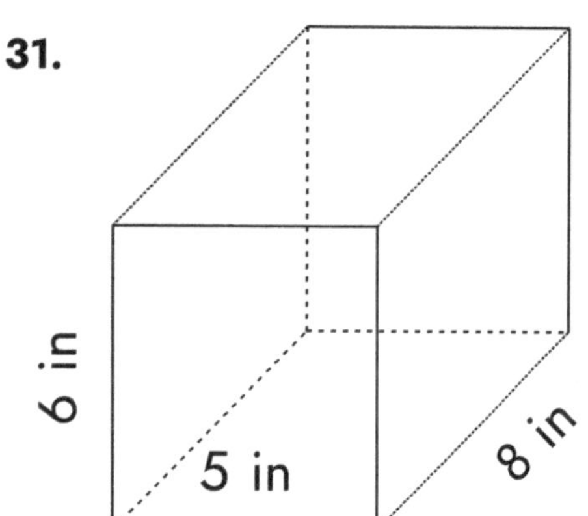

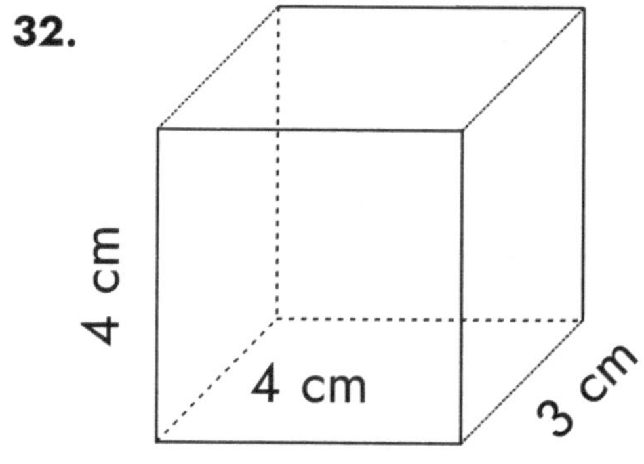

<u>Statistics</u>

<u>Mean</u>

The mean, also known as the average, is a measure of central tendency.

To find the mean of a set of numbers:

- Add up all the numbers in the set.
- Divide the sum by the total count of numbers in the set.

For example: consider the set of numbers: 70, 72, 49, 69, 27, 76.

$$\text{Mean} = \frac{70 + 72 + 49 + 69 + 27 + 76}{6}$$

$$= \frac{363}{6} = 60.5$$

<u>Median</u>

The median is a measure of central tendency that represents the middle value of a dataset when the values are arranged in ascending or descending order.

To find the median of a set of numbers:

- Arrange the numbers in ascending or descending order.
- If the total count of numbers is odd, the median is the middle value.
- If the total count of numbers is even, the median is the average of the two middle values.

For example: consider the set of numbers: 70, 72, 49, 69, 27, 76.

$$27, 49, 69, 70, 72, 76$$

$$\text{Median} = \frac{69 + 70}{2} = \frac{139}{2} = 69.5$$

Mode

The mode in statistics refers to the value that appears most frequently in a given set of data.

Let's consider the following set of numbers:

$$\{2, 4, 4, 5, 6, 6, 6, 7, 8, 8\}$$

In this set, the number 6 appears three times, more than any other number. Therefore, the mode of this dataset is 6.

It's possible for a dataset to have more than one mode if two or more numbers appear with the same highest frequency. In such cases, the dataset is considered multimodal. If no number repeats, the dataset is considered to have no mode.

For example:

$$\{2, 4, 4, 4, 5, 6, 6, 6, 7, 8, 8\}$$

In this date set, 4 and 6 appear three times. Therefore, this dataset is multimodal.

Range

In statistics, the range refers to the difference between the largest and smallest values in a dataset. It represents the spread or variability of the data.

For example, consider the dataset { 68, 13, 30, 18, 45, 76, 11}:

To calculate the range:

1. Arrange the data points in ascending order.

$$11, 13, 18, 30, 45, 68, 76$$

2. Subtract the smallest value from the largest value.

- The smallest value is 11.
- The largest value is 76.

$$\text{Range} = \text{Largest value} - \text{smallest value} = 76 - 11 = 65.$$

Mean, Median, Mode, and Range

Find the Mean, Median, Mode and Range of the following sets of data.

1. 9, 30, 7, 91, 12, 61, 35

   Mean = _____   Median = _____

   Mode = _____   Range = _____

2. 82, 40, 79, 93, 47, 38

   Mean = _____   Median = _____

   Mode = _____   Range = _____

3. 46, 24, 58, 67, 43, 32

   Mean = _____   Median = _____

   Mode = _____   Range = _____

4. 32, 87, 97, 57, 13, 9, 29

Mean = _______   Median = _____

Mode = _______   Range = _____

5. 84, 76, 33, 70, 88, 23

Mean = _______   Median = _____

Mode = _______   Range = _____

6. 45, 64, 57, 81, 56, 90, 48

Mean = _____   Median = _____

Mode = _____   Range = _____

7. 31, 50, 78, 65, 28, 55, 84

Mean = _______   Median = _____

Mode = _______   Range = _____

8. 11, 11, 61, 45, 25, 35

Mean = _______   Median = _____

Mode = _______   Range = _____

9. 52, 12, 31, 12, 73, 93

Mean = _____   Median = _____

Mode = _____   Range = _____

10. 83, 82, 77, 58, 50, 69, 91

Mean = _______   Median = _____

Mode = _______   Range = _____

11. 71, 3, 73, 88, 42, 3

Mean = _______   Median = _____

Mode = _______   Range = _____

12. 77, 94, 2, 82, 9, 32

Mean = _______   Median = _____

Mode = _______   Range = _____

13. 29, 58, 25, 19, 73, 16, 87

Mean = _______   Median = _____

Mode = _______   Range = _____

14. 46, 54, 70, 33, 34, 46, 9

Mean = _______   Median = _____

Mode = _______   Range = _____

15. 62, 8, 66, 53, 91, 28, 95

Mean = _______   Median = _____

Mode = _______   Range = _____

16. 37, 84, 81, 37, 23, 20

Mean = _____   Median = _____

Mode = _____   Range = _____

17. 42, 48, 40, 51, 30, 22, 79

Mean = _______   Median = _____

Mode = _______   Range = _____

18. 44, 36, 58, 64, 4, 43

Mean = _____   Median = _____

Mode = _____   Range = _____

19. 62, 24, 37, 1, 69, 40, 43

Mean = _______   Median = _____

Mode = _______   Range = _____

20. 34, 41, 69, 28, 48, 90, 80

Mean = _______   Median = _____

Mode = _______   Range = _____

21. 37, 92, 74, 43, 81, 51

Mean = _____   Median = _____

Mode = _____   Range = _____

22. 96, 46, 98, 14, 20, 3

Mean = _______   Median = _____

Mode = _______   Range = _____

23. 12, 67, 64, 26, 49, 3, 50

Mean = _______   Median = _____

Mode = _______   Range = _____

ANSWERS

Page 1: Exponents

1. 1/125   **2.** 1/2744   **3.** 1/64   **4.** 49   **5.** 27

6. 1/49   **7.** 28,561   **8.** 1,728   **9.** 6,859   **10.** 729

11. 1/100   **12.** 1/256   **13.** 83,521   **14.** 9   **15.** 1/324

16. 1/1000   **17.** 36   **18.** 1/169   **19.** 1/196   **20.** 361

21. 1/729   **22.** 343   **23.** 1   **24.** 1/5832   **25.** 10,000

26. 5,832   **27.** 14,641   **28.** 160,000   **29.** 4,913   **30.** 1/2197

Page 4: Square and Cube Roots

1. 20   **2.** 10   **3.** 11   **4.** 8   **5.** 4   **6.** 3   **7.** 19   **8.** 31   **9.** 1

10. 23   **11.** 3   **12.** 4   **13.** 10   **14.** 12   **15.** 2   **16.** 2   **17.** 6   **18.** 11

19. 18   **20.** 99   **21.** 5   **22.** 6   **23.** 47   **24.** 24   **25.** 90   **26.** 22   **27.** 8

28. 56   **29.** 13   **30.** 77   **31.** 9   **32.** 1   **33.** 9   **34.** 14   **35.** 17   **36.** 93

Page 7: Factors

1. 2, 4, 7, 14

2. 2, 4

3. 2, 5, 7, 10, 14, 35

4. None

5. None

6. 2, 3, 6, 7, 14, 21

7. 2, 3

8. 3, 5, 15, 25

9. 2, 4, 8, 11, 22, 44

10. 3

11. 2, 47

12. 2, 3, 4, 6, 7, 12, 14, 21, 28, 42

13. 2, 3, 4, 6, 8, 12, 16, 24, 32, 48

14. 2, 3, 6, 11, 22, 33

15. 2, 3, 4, 6, 8, 12, 16, 24

16. 2, 7, 14, 49

17. None

18. None

19. 2, 4, 5, 10

20. 5, 11

21. 2, 3, 4, 6

22. None

23. 2, 7

24. 2, 4, 11, 22

25. 3, 7, 9, 21

26. 5, 13

27. 3, 5

28. None

Page 11: Multiples

1. 23, 46, 69, 92, 115

2. 15, 30, 45, 60, 75

3. 22, 44, 66, 88, 110

4. 4, 8, 12, 16, 20

5. 81, 162, 243, 324, 405

6. 95, 190, 285, 380, 475

7. 87, 174, 261, 348, 435

8. 48, 96, 144, 192, 240

9. 38, 76, 114, 152, 190

10. 2, 4, 6, 8, 10

11. 60, 120, 180, 240, 300

12. 3, 6, 9, 12, 15

13. 1, 2, 3, 4, 5

14. 20, 40, 60, 80, 100

15. 7, 14, 21, 28, 35

16. 59, 118, 177, 236, 295

17. 70, 140, 210, 280, 350

18. 9, 18, 27, 36, 45

19. 28, 56, 84, 112, 140

20. 14, 28, 42, 56, 70

21. 18, 36, 54, 72, 90

22. 61, 122, 183, 244, 305

23. 6, 12, 18, 24, 30

24. 10, 20, 30, 40, 50

25. 8, 16, 24, 32, 40

26. 34, 68, 102, 136, 170

27. 30, 60, 90, 120, 150

28. 84, 168, 252, 336, 420

Page 15: Greatest Common Factor

1. 28   **2.** 3   **3.** 12   **4.** 2   **5.** 11   **6.** 22   **7.** 2   **8.** 22   **9.** 11   **10.** 11

11. 11   **12.** 3   **13.** 9   **14.** 3   **15.** 6   **16.** 10   **17.** 2   **18.** 11   **19.** 5   **20.** 5

21. 7   **22.** 2   **23.** 21

Page 19: Prime Numbers

1. 2×19 (No)   **2.** 7 (Yes)   **3.** 7×7 (No)

4. 19 (Yes)   **5.** 3×3 (No)   **6.** 2×2 (No)

7. 83 (Yes)   **8.** 2×23 (No)   **9.** 89 (Yes)

10. 1 (No)   **11.** 2×3×13 (No)   **12.** 43 (Yes)

13. 2×2×2×2×2×2 (No)   **14.** 3 (Yes)   **15.** 2×29 (No)

16. 5×7 (No)   **17.** 2×11 (No)   **18.** 2×2×2×11 (No)

19. 2×13 (No)   **20.** 2×3×3×3 (No)   **21.** 79 (Yes)

22. 2×2×3×3 (No)   **23.** 2×2×2 (No)   **24.** 2×2×2×2×3 (No)

25. 2×3 (No)   **26.** 17 (Yes)   **27.** 3×3×7 (No)

28. 3×29 (No)   **29.** 5×5 (No)   **30.** 2×2×2×2×2×3 (No)

Page 21: Positive and Negative Integers

1. 1   **2.** -8   **3.** -6   **4.** -18   **5.** 1   **6.** -3   **7.** 9   **8.** 5   **9.** 5

10. -13   **11.** -24   **12.** 3   **13.** 3   **14.** -8   **15.** -8   **16.** 10   **17.** -4   **18.** 0

19. -17   **20.** 14   **21.** -25   **22.** -3   **23.** -5   **24.** 2   **25.** -9   **26.** -12   **27.** 6

28. 5

Page 24: Order of Operations (PEMDAS)

1. 9   **2.** 18   **3.** 23   **4.** 23   **5.** 26   **6.** 34   **7.** 14   **8.** 12   **9.** 21

10. 24   **11.** 19   **12.** 8   **13.** 16   **14.** 32   **15.** 10   **16.** 22   **17.** 12   **18.** 9

19. 23   **20.** 15   **21.** 19   **22.** 20   **23.** 26   **24.** 15   **25.** 9   **26.** 8   **27.** 26

28. 13

Page 27: Solving Equations: (One Side)

1. $x = 4$ **2.** $x = 4$ **3.** $x = 19$ **4.** $x = 9$ **5.** $x = 18$ **6.** $x = 9$

7. $x = 8$ **8.** $x = 8$ **9.** $x = 13$ **10.** $x = 2$ **11.** $x = 10$ **12.** $x = 12$

13. $x = 2$ **14.** $x = 7$ **15.** $x = 12$ **16.** $x = 14$ **17.** $x = 15$ **18.** $x = 16$

19. $x = 10$ **20.** $x = 15$ **21.** $x = 7$ **22.** $x = 18$ **23.** $x = 2$ **24.** $x = 14$

25. $x = 10$ **26.** $x = 12$ **27.** $x = 14$ **28.** $x = 3$

Page 30: One-Step Equations

1. 5   **2.** 6   **3.** 10   **4.** 7   **5.** 7   **6.** 4   **7.** 9   **8.** 2   **9.** 7

10. 9   **11.** 7   **12.** 7   **13.** 8   **14.** 5   **15.** 1   **16.** 8   **17.** 9   **18.** 6

19. 9   **20.** 9   **21.** 8   **22.** 2   **23.** 6   **24.** 4   **25.** 9   **26.** 10   **27.** 10

28. 9   **29.** 6   **30.** 4   **31.** 6   **32.** 7

Page 34: Two-Step Equations

1. 1   **2.** 3   **3.** 6   **4.** 7   **5.** 3

6. 8   **7.** 2 or -2   **8.** 4   **9.** 8   **10.** 5

11. 2   **12.** 2   **13.** 2   **14.** 2   **15.** 6

16. 10 or -11   **17.** 3   **18.** 7   **19.** 5   **20.** 2

21. 6   **22.** 8   **23.** 5   **24.** 1   **25.** 10

26. 10   **27.** 8   **28.** 9   **29.** 1   **30.** 7

31. 8   **32.** 3

Page 38:   Solving Inequalities

1. $z < -1$ **2.** $x < -1$ **3.** $z \geq 2$ **4.** $z \leq -6$ **5.** $z \leq -2$ **6.** $x \leq -4$

7. $z > -15$ **8.** $x > 3$ **9.** $k < -5$ **10.** $x \leq -1$ **11.** $z \leq -12$ **12.** $x < -5$

13. $x \leq -3$ **14.** $m \geq -1$ **15.** $x \leq 0$ **16.** $k > -1$ **17.** $z > -7$ **18.** $k \leq 13$

19. $m < -11$ **20.** $z \leq -1$

Page 43:   Proportional Relationship

1. 24   **2.** 5   **3.** 1   **4.** 63   **5.** 3   **6.** 16   **7.** 7   **8.** 12   **9.** 4

10. 81   **11.** 1   **12.** 45   **13.** 11   **14.** 36   **15.** 12   **16.** 6   **17.** 5   **18.** 2

19. 12   **20.** 4   **21.** 49   **22.** 99   **23.** 2   **24.** 81   **25.** 5   **26.** 4   **27.** 2

28. 70   **29.** 5   **30.** 1   **31.** 36   **32.** 20

Page 46:   Percentage

1. 600   **2.** 60   **3.** 20%   **4.** 125   **5.** 300   **6.** 900   **7.** 35%   **8.** 2400

9. 600   **10.** 270   **11.** 40   **12.** 42   **13.** 72   **14.** 1%   **15.** 630   **16.** 50%

17. 80   **18.** 200   **19.** 500   **20.** 2   **21.** 4%   **22.** 5   **23.** 18   **24.** 800

25. 40   **26.** 6%   **27.** 70%   **28.** 5%   **29.** 400   **30.** 400   **31.** 10   **32.** 35%

33. 500   **34.** 10%

Page 49:   Convert Percent and Decimals

1. 85%   **2.** 0.51   **3.** 44%   **4.** 0.68   **5.** 21%   **6.** 0.11   **7.** 47%

8. 25%   **9.** 0.39   **10.** 0.62   **11.** 63%   **12.** 87%   **13.** 34%   **14.** 36%

15. 48%   **16.** 10%   **17.** 0.02   **18.** 64%   **19.** 1   **20.** 0.07   **21.** 15%

22. 0.18   **23.** 0.76   **24.** 0.94   **25.** 0.72   **26.** 0.14   **27.** 49%   **28.** 35%

29. 46%   **30.** 71%   **31.** 16%   **32.** 0.31   **33.** 75%   **34.** 0.41

Page 52: Convert: Ratio, Fraction, Percent, and Decimals

1.

	Ratio	Fraction	Percent	Decimal
a.	1:8	1/8	12.5%	0.125
b.	1:1	1/1	100%	1
c.	16:18	16/18	88.9%	0.889
d.	12:15	12/15	80%	0.8
e.	11:14	11/14	78.6%	0.786
f.	2:3	2/3	66.7%	0.667
g.	1:2	1/2	50%	0.5
h.	5:8	5/8	62.5%	0.625
i.	1:4	1/4	25%	0.25
j.	9:20	9/20	45%	0.45
k.	1:13	1/13	7.7%	0.077
l.	3:5	3/5	60%	0.6
m.	7:18	7/18	38.9%	0.389
n.	9:10	9/10	90%	0.9
o.	6:20	6/20	30%	0.3

2.

	Ratio	Fraction	Percent	Decimal
a.	2:2	2/2	100%	1
b.	12:14	12/14	85.7%	0.857
c.	6:16	6/16	37.5%	0.375
d.	2:15	2/15	13.3%	0.133
e.	17:19	17/19	89.5%	0.895
f.	5:9	5/9	55.6%	0.556
g.	4:5	4/5	80%	0.8
h.	2:11	2/11	18.2%	0.182
i.	16:18	16/18	88.9%	0.889
j.	6:17	6/17	35.3%	0.353
k.	15:17	15/17	88.2%	0.882
l.	3:12	3/12	25%	0.25
m.	3:11	3/11	27.3%	0.273
n.	1:4	1/4	25%	0.25
o.	2:10	2/10	20%	0.2

3.

	Ratio	Fraction	Percent	Decimal
a.	2:10	2/10	20%	0.2
b.	4:13	4/13	30.8%	0.308
c.	14:19	14/19	73.7%	0.737
d.	15:17	15/17	88.2%	0.882
e.	2:14	2/14	14.3%	0.143
f.	3:11	3/11	27.3%	0.273
g.	2:8	2/8	25%	0.25
h.	1:17	1/17	5.9%	0.059
i.	15:15	15/15	100%	1
j.	11:19	11/19	57.9%	0.579
k.	6:12	6/12	50%	0.5
l.	2:16	2/16	12.5%	0.125
m.	6:7	6/7	85.7%	0.857
n.	3:9	3/9	33.3%	0.333
o.	16:17	16/17	94.1%	0.941

Page 55: Area and Perimeter

1. P=78 A=208

2. P=44 A=91

3. P=60 A=168

4. P=28 A=49

5. P=30 A=43.3

6. P=45 A=95.03

7. P=37 A=48.96

8. P=64 A=225

9. P=54 A=118

10. P=43 A=78

11. P=43 A=78

12. P=18 A=15.59

13. P=34 A=50

14. P=22 A=30

15. P=30 A=25.2

16. P=29 A=32.4

17. P=50 A=156

18. P=40 A=36

19. P=42 A=86

20. P=51 A=112

21. P=36 A=70

22. P=62 A=240

23. P=60 A=125

24. P=21 A=18

25. P=22 A=30

26. P=23 A=25.16

27. P=42 A=52

28. P=27 A=35.07

Page 62: Classify and Measure Angles

1. 270° Reflex

2. 80° Acute

3. 235° Reflex

4. 205° Reflex

5. 100° Obtuse

6. 180° Straight

7. 280° Reflex

8. 190° Reflex

9. 40° Acute

10. 295° Reflex

11. 215° Reflex

12. 210° Reflex

13. 315° Reflex	**14.** 140° Obtuse	**15.** 305° Reflex	**16.** 355° Reflex
17. 140° Obtuse	**18.** 5° Acute	**19.** 5° Acute	**20.** 155° Obtuse
21. 185° Reflex	**22.** 75° Acute	**23.** 180° Straight	**24.** 65° Acute

Page 68: Volume and Surface Area

1. $V=8$ ft³ ft³ SA=24 ft² ft²

2. $V=168$ ft³ ft³ SA=188 ft² ft²

3. $V=48$ in³ in³ SA=80 in² in²

4. $V=448$ cm³ cm³ SA=352 cm² cm²

5. $V=216$ ft³ ft³ SA=216 ft² ft²

6. $V=150$ in³ in³ SA=170 in² in²

7. $V=324$ in³ in³ SA=288 in² in²

8. $V=693$ in³ in³ SA=478 in² in²

9. $V=252$ in³ in³ SA=240 in² in²

10. $V=560$ cm³ cm³ SA=412 cm² cm²

11. $V=113.10$ cm³ cm³ SA=132 cm² cm²

12. $V=18$ ft³ ft³ SA=42 ft² ft²

13. $V=75.40$ ft³ ft³ SA=101 ft² ft²

14. $V=270$ in³ in³ SA=258 in² in²

15. $V=150$ ft³ ft³ SA=170 ft² ft²

16. $V=21.21$ in³ in³ SA=42 in² in²

17. $V=78.54$ cm³ cm³ SA=102 cm² cm²

18. $V=567$ in³ in³ SA=414 in² in²

19. $V=197.92$ cm³ cm³ SA=188 cm² cm²

20. $V=117.81$ ft³ ft³ SA=134 ft² ft²

21. $V=855.30$ ft³ ft³ SA=501 ft² ft²

22. $V=360$ ft³ ft³ SA=312 ft² ft²

23. $V=252$ cm³ cm³ SA=240 cm² cm²

24. $V=18$ ft³ ft³ SA=42 ft² ft²

25. $V=12$ cm³ cm³ SA=32 cm² cm²

26. $V=700$ cm³ cm³ SA=480 cm² cm²

27. $V=448$ in³ in³ SA=352 in² in²

28. $V=226.19$ in³ in³ SA=207 in² in²

29. $V=48$ in³ in³ SA=80 in² in²

30. $V=508.94$ ft³ ft³ SA=353 ft² ft²

31. $V=240$ in³ in³ SA=236 in² in²

32. $V=48$ cm³ cm³ SA=80 cm² cm²

Page 76: Mean, Median, Mode, and Range

1. Mean = 35, Median = 30, Mode = none, Range = 84

2. Mean = 63.167, Median = 63, Mode = none, Range = 55

3. Mean = 45, Median = 44.5, Mode = none, Range = 43

4. Mean = 46.286, Median = 32, Mode = none, Range = 88

5. Mean = 62.333, Median = 73, Mode = none, Range = 65

6. Mean = 63, Median = 57, Mode = none, Range = 45

7. Mean = 55.857, Median = 55, Mode = none, Range = 56

8. Mean = 31.333, Median = 30, Mode = 11, Range = 50

9. Mean = 45.5, Median = 41.5, Mode = 12, Range = 81

10. Mean = 72.857, Median = 77, Mode = none, Range = 41

11. Mean = 46.667, Median = 56.5, Mode = 3, Range = 85

12. Mean = 49.333, Median = 54.5, Mode = none, Range = 92

13. Mean = 43.857, Median = 29, Mode = none, Range = 71

14. Mean = 41.714, Median = 46, Mode = 46, Range = 61

15. Mean = 57.571, Median = 62, Mode = none, Range = 87

16. Mean = 47, Median = 37, Mode = 37, Range = 64

17. Mean = 44.571, Median = 42, Mode = none, Range = 57

18. Mean = 41.5, Median = 43.5, Mode = none, Range = 60

19. Mean = 39.429, Median = 40, Mode = none, Range = 68

20. Mean = 55.714, Median = 48, Mode = none, Range = 62

21. Mean = 63, Median = 62.5, Mode = none, Range = 55

22. Mean = 46.167, Median = 33, Mode = none, Range = 95

23. Mean = 38.714, Median = 49, Mode = none, Range = 64